THE SPANISH INQUISITION

The
Spanish Inquisition

A. S. TURBERVILLE

ARCHON BOOKS
1968

First published 1932

Reprinted 1968 with permission of
Oxford University Press
in an unaltered and unabridged edition

Library of Congress Catalog Card Number: 68-11257
Printed in the United States of America

CONTENTS

CHAPTER I

THE MEDIEVAL INQUISITION AND MEDIEVAL SPAIN

THE fame of the Spanish Inquisition as it was established by Ferdinand and Isabella towards the close of the fifteenth century has been such that it has tended to blur popular recognition of the fact that the Holy Office was active in many other countries besides Spain, and existed long before the fifteenth century. It is true that the Spanish tribunal had distinctive characteristics which justify the treatment of it as a separate institution, but it is not possible to appreciate its peculiarities without reference to the Inquisition in other lands and at other periods.

The Inquisition was evolved in the Middle Ages as an effective means of coping with the problem of heresy, which became a serious menace to the Catholic Church in the twelfth century. The literal meaning of the word heresy is choosing, selecting, and of the heinousness of the

1

sin of selecting beliefs instead of obediently accepting the whole faith of the Church there was in that era no gainsaying, save indeed by the heretics themselves. Though there had been differences of view among the early Christian Fathers as to the proper methods of dealing with the heretic, there was no doubt as to his culpability, and Polycarp speaks of him as antichrist, the first son of the Devil. Thomas Aquinas in his *Summa Theologica*, the supreme monument of thirteenth-century learning, likens the heretic to the false coiner. As the latter corrupts the currency, which is necessary for the temporal life, so the heretic corrupts the faith, which is necessary for the life of the soul. Death is the penalty which is justly meted out by the secular prince to the coiner, and death therefore must be the rightful reward of the heretic, whose offence is as much graver as the life of the soul is more precious than that of the body.

Such reasoning is based upon two cardinal assumptions, which it is all-important to grasp if the Inquisition is to be understood. The first is that there exists a *Respublica Christiana*, a single Christian society, just as there exists a single

2

Catholic Church, and that both Church and State have the truths of the Christian religion as their essential foundation. The second is that the security of the body politic and ecclesiastical calls for discipline both in Church and State, for the obedience of the subject to his lawful rulers, civil and hierarchical. The heretic is, then, just as much as the criminal, a rebel and a pariah.

It is an error to think of the persecution of heretics as being forced by the Church upon unwilling or indifferent laity. The heretic was an unpopular person in the Middle Ages. There are, in fact, instances in the late eleventh century and early twelfth century of heretics being lynched by an infuriated mob, who regarded the clergy as too lenient ; and the secular authorities as a rule co-operated very readily with the ecclesiastical in endeavouring to root out an evil which was looked upon as dangerous to sound morals as well as to sound doctrine—for a corrupt tree brings forth corrupt fruit, and a man who believes falsely will act wrongly. In 1184 there took place a very important conference in Verona between Pope Lucius III and the Emperor Frederick Barbarossa, at which the supreme

pontiff and the supreme secular over-
lord of Christendom agreed to co-operate
against heresy and decided that the ultimate penalties for obduracy in this crime
should be exile and confiscation of property. In 1197 King Pedro II of Aragon
went further than this. He decreed that
banishment should be the penalty for
heresy, but added that if the culprit remained within his dominions in defiance
of the edict he should be put to death.
In a Constitution issued for Lombardy by
the Emperor Frederick II in 1220 the
penalties prescribed for heresy were those
agreed upon at the Verona conference;
but in 1224 the cutting out of the tongue
or death at the stake was ordained. In
the Constitutions of Melfi, which applied
only to the island of Sicily, the Emperor
omitted the milder alternative; and in
1238 he enforced death by burning as the
punishment of heresy upon Germany.
The *Établissements* of Louis IX (1270)
similarly made the stake the lawful penalty
for heresy in France. A hundred and
thirty years later, in 1401, the same death
for this offence became part of the law
of England by the statute *De Heretico
Comburendo*.

It was, then, the generally accepted

4

view, held by the laity as well as by the clergy in medieval Christendom (except, of course, in those comparatively few communities in which heresy was so rampant as to obtain the upper hand, notably in Languedoc in the second half of the twelfth century), that heresy was the most heinous of crimes, justly punished by the most dreadful of deaths. But it is, on the other hand, necessary to add that this widespread conviction was the result of the teaching of the Church, which was primarily concerned with the offence of error in belief. The ordinary uninstructed layman had little knowledge of theology, and was not in a position, save in the quite obvious cases, to distinguish between the orthodox and the heterodox, which was often a matter of no little subtlety. It is one thing to be conscious of the enormity of error; it is quite another thing to detect error. Thus the secular arm was competent to punish heresy, but it was not competent to investigate it, being unequipped with the necessary technical knowledge. Hence the search for, and the trial of, heretics was the concern of the appropriate ecclesiastical authority, and the appropriate ecclesiastical authority was that of the bishop,

5

who dealt with the offence of heresy as well as with multifarious other ecclesiastical offences in his diocesan court.

It is important to notice that at no time was the responsibility of the bishop with regard to heresy removed ; but early in the thirteenth century it was already apparent that the machinery of episcopal control was quite inadequate to deal with such widespread and formidable heretical movements as those of Catharism and Waldensianism, which had become very serious, especially in southern France and northern Italy, but also in Germany and other countries as well. It was in the territories of the Counts of Toulouse that the situation was most alarming, and the famous attempt to extirpate the heretics of that region by force of arms in the Albigensian Crusades, which were undertaken at the behest of Pope Innocent III, is the classical example of completely successful persecution. Recourse was had to military effort because of the failure alike of missionary enterprise to reconvert the erring and of episcopal justice to punish the obdurate ; but military effort would not have achieved such phenomenal success had it been unaided. The Albigensian Crusades were triumphant largely because they paved the way for the introduction into the Languedoc country of an effective organization for the combating of heresy which remained there long after the crusaders had gone. The organization was that of the Inquisition.

The deficiencies of the machinery which the bishop had at his disposal for dealing with heresy are manifest. In the first place, his authority was limited to his own diocese and was therefore too circumscribed to enable him to cope effectively with a problem which was international. In the second place, his duties were too onerous and too multifarious to allow of his bestowing the amount of time and the unremitting care to this one particular task which its magnitude and its urgency alike demanded. Indeed the bishops are described as oppressed by " a whirlwind of cares " and " overwhelming anxieties " in a most important letter of Pope Gregory IX of April 1233, in which he explains that in view of these distractions he has decided to send the Dominicans or Preaching Friars to do battle with the heretics of France. In so far as it is legitimate to ascribe the origin of such an institution to any one man and to a particular date, the origin of the Inquisition may be assigned to Gregory IX and to this year 1233. For Gregory had perceived in the existence of the two great Mendicant orders the opportunity of creating an expert force of trained men for the special service of attacking heresy. They were, indeed, exceptionally well fitted for the task by their freedom from monastic or parochial ties, their high and as yet untarnished ideals of devotion to the spirit of their founders, their zeal for missionary enterprise, and the intellectual eminence of many of their members, especially among the Prædicants. The Friars were to co-operate with the bishops as experts in the investigation and the trial of cases of heretical pravity. To start with, their authority was regarded as co-ordinate with that of the bishops, but before long the latter inevitably tended to fall into the background despite the protests of the more energetic among them, who were inclined to resent what they regarded as an encroachment upon their powers. Specialists who were devoting their whole time, thought and energy to a single purpose were bound to obtain the effective control, since they came to develop a distinctive technique and a definite body of juridical principles. In the newly

8

created tribunals for the trial of heresy and of other offences in which heresy was implicit the central presiding figure was not the bishop, but the friar-inquisitor.

Why do we speak of this court for the trial of heresy, the Holy Office as it is properly named, as the Inquisition ; why is its chief official, who acts as the judge, known as an inquisitor ? The answer is that the inquisitor was not solely a judge and that his duties were by no means confined within the walls of the tribunal. He was also an investigator, and he and his assistants were occupied, not only in the judicial function of pronouncing judgment upon the criminal, but also in the police function of bringing him to judgment. The word Inquisition also has reference to the method by which this process was accomplished. The normal procedure in the ordinary ecclesiastical courts was either by the *denuntiatio* of an archdeacon or by the *accusatio* of a private individual who proffered information from his own personal knowledge. Neither method proved adequate in dealing with heresy in the thirteenth century. The duties of the archdeacon were manifold, and it could not be expected that any large number of heretics would be

9

brought to justice by his instrumentality ; and the method of trusting to the activities of the private individual was altogether too haphazard. He was apt to be too indifferent to come forward in districts where heresy was not very widespread and to be restrained by fear of reprisals in districts where it was deeply rooted. The fact was that in their campaign against heretical pravity the authorities were hampered by lack of a police force.

How was this deficiency to be made good ? In the Edict of Verona (1184) the bishops were instructed to make periodical visitations of parishes within their dioceses in which heresy was supposed to exist, and to compel residents of trustworthy character or even the entire population to name any persons in their midst whose manner of life differed suspiciously from that of good Catholics. This system was improved upon when in 1227 a Council at Narbonne decided that bishops should appoint in each of their parishes *testes synodales* (synodal witnesses), whose duty it would be to inquire diligently concerning heresy and give information to their bishops. In this way a sort of unofficial police was created for the express purpose of ferreting out heretics, and the author-

10

ities became possessed of the *diffamatio* of each neighbourhood against persons popularly regarded as objects of suspicion. Upon such a groundwork of delation, of specific denunciation in some cases, of mere rumour in others, the inquisitor was able to make headway. He was much assisted by his familiars or agents, who could be utilized as detectives, and by the device of proclaiming a " time of grace," i.e. of granting to the heretic who surrendered himself within the allotted period and gave information not only against himself but against his accomplices, either complete exemption from, or considerable mitigation of, the penalties which he had incurred. This process of preliminary investigation was technically known as the *inquisitio generalis*. It was succeeded by the *inquisitio specialis* or actual trial of the persons incriminated therein, and in the trial the inquisitor appeared in the twofold capacity of accuser and judge, this anomalous combination of incompatible functions, as it seems to us, being accounted for by the fact that the inquisitor did not regard himself as either accuser or judge, but simply as a father-confessor seeking to bring the erring to repentance and imposing the penance appropriate to the fault acknowledged. The Spanish Inquisition of later times, as we shall see, followed these methods of the medieval tribunals with the exception that it employed a prosecuting officer to prefer a definite charge against the accuser, so that the inquisitor's position was, ostensibly at all events, less ambiguous.

The medieval Inquisition was essentially an institution devised by the Papacy and controlled by it; but in France, at all events, it had to reckon with the power of the Crown. Incidentally, its labours in Languedoc aided the aggrandisement of the French monarchy by bringing into complete subjection to the King territories which had hitherto been the virtually independent possession of the Counts of Toulouse. As the strength of the monarchy increased and as that of the Papacy, discredited by the Babylonish Captivity and the subsequent scandal of the Schism, declined, so the influence of the Inquisition in the country was prejudiced, until in the days of Calvinism one finds the repression of heresy being undertaken, not by the Inquisition but by the University of Paris, with its great tradition of theological learning, and by a special chamber

12

of the *Parlement*, known as the *Chambre Ardente*.

The medieval Inquisition, controlled by an international authority, was international also in its province. It penetrated into many countries—even into eastern Europe beyond the Adriatic, but it never secured sure foothold there, and it was a really effective force in western Europe only. It accomplished little in Hungary, Bohemia and Poland ; it never entered Scandinavia. In England it appeared only once—in 1309—when special papal commissioneries undertook, in concert with the native episcopal authority, proceedings against the English Templars, the whole Order having been defamed of heresy. They found themselves hampered by the non-employment of torture in the country, but even when given special permission by Edward II to make use of it, they made slow progress. It was in France, in Germany and in Italy that the medieval Inquisition was most energetic and powerful. But everywhere the papal Inquisition was either virtually extinct or moribund at the time when Ferdinand and Isabella gave a new lease to inquisitorial activity. The Holy Office received a new impetus also in Italy some sixty years later, the revival of the papal Inquisition in Rome being one of the outstanding facts of the Counter-Reformation. One of the most famous of the popes of that period, Pius V, had been a very zealous inquisitor before his elevation to the pontificate. Both in Spain and in Rome the modern Inquisitions were partly new creations, partly revivals. Ferdinand and Isabella did not start upon absolutely virgin soil. The papal Inquisition had entered Spain in the Middle Ages, but for reasons which it is essential to appreciate it had not been a flourishing institution in that country.

Spain was a purely geographical term in the Middle Ages. It had been a very important province of the Roman Empire, producing some of the finest Latin writers of the silver age, and providing some of the most efficient man-power for the legions. In the fifth century the barbarians had descended upon the country —Alani, Suevi, and Vandals, doing great damage but making no permanent settlement; more important were the Visigoths, who made peace with the Roman emperors and controlled Spain in their name. Vir-

tually there existed a Visigothic kingdom
of Spain, until the beginning of the eighth
century, when there appeared new invaders
—Berbers from northern Africa.

Thus a Mohammedan civilization was
introduced, and Caliphs of Arab race
reigned at Córdova until 1031. In many
of the arts and sciences Saracen Spain
was more advanced than the Christian
people of western Europe, notably in
medicine and mathematics, while its archi-
tecture, though not of the highest order,
had a charm which survives to this day.
The rule of the Moors was, on the whole,
distinctly beneficent ; unlike the Ottoman
Turks they were not as a rule fanatical
Muslims. There were many conversions
among the Christian people to Islam, and
there was much intermarriage between the
two races. The great Ommayad dynasty
reached the zenith of its power in the
middle of the tenth century ; after that
there was declension, and the united
Moorish State became disintegrated. In
the eleventh, twelfth and thirteenth centuries the Peninsula was gradually won
back for Christianity.

The hold of the Moors did not extend
into the extreme north of Spain, into the
regions of the Biscay coast, of the Cant-

abrian Mountains and the Pyrenees. At the opening of the eleventh century the Christian reconquest was begun by Sancho of Navarre; his son Ferdinand I, " the Great," who became ruler of the kingdoms of Leon and Castile, captured the great Moorish city of Toledo and brought his effective power as far south as the Tagus. The wars of his son Alfonso VI are associated with the semi-mythical figure of The Cid, who, though he appears in poetry and legend as the perfect knight of Christian chivalry, seems in reality to have been a free-lance fighting always for his own hand, quite prepared to assist the Moors when it seemed to be to his own advantage. These religious wars were, indeed, waged with very little religious bitterness. Of various small Christian kingdoms two came to predominate over the rest—Castile, which absorbed Leon; Aragon, which absorbed Catalonia. In 1212 allied Aragonese and Castilian forces, aided by a motley crew of crusaders from other lands, won a resounding victory over the Moors at Las Navas de Tolosa, south of the Sierra Morena. Ferdinand III of Castile (1217–52) extended his conquests as far south as Córdova and Seville, which had been the very centres of Moorish power. James the Conqueror of Aragon (1213–76) added the Balearic Isles and Valencia to his kingdom. By the opening of the fourteenth century Muslim Spain was reduced to the kingdom of Granada.

In the later Middle Ages the history of Spain is extremely disjointed, there being no such central theme as that of the Christian reconquest to give it unity and interest. In the fourteenth century the crown of Castile was worn by weak and worthless rulers, such as the feeble and nerveless John II, and his utterly decadent successor, Henry IV, " El Impotente." The history of Aragon during the same period was no less unsatisfactory, the power of the monarchy being severely limited by the inordinate privileges enjoyed by the nobles and the very considerable powers possessed by the Cortes of Aragon, Catalonia and Valencia. But in 1474 Isabella came to the throne of Castile, and five years later her husband Ferdinand became King of Aragon, and a new era dawned. The union between the two kingdoms brought about by this marriage alliance was personal only ; in many respects their interests remained quite dissimilar. But the royal marriage

17

was much more than a mere symbol of concord; it meant unity of policy and the pooling of resources; it was the making of modern Spain.

The problem of creating some sort of national and political union in the country continued for a long time to be one of the utmost difficulty. That considerable progress was made during the reigns of Ferdinand and Isabella is an indication not only of the practical value of their marriage in the interests of the country, but also of their altogether remarkable ability. Extraordinary diversities of character existed between the different peoples of Spain—between Castilians, Galicians, Catalans, Valencians, Andalusians, etc. There were, too, radical differences of race and religion. For many centuries Jews had formed a large proportion of the population; there were also the Moors, spread abroad like the Jews in all parts of the country, though most numerous in the south and east. Right in the south there still existed the separate Muslim kingdom of Granada. Till that kingdom had been subdued, the Christian reconquest of Spain was not complete. With so many Mohammedans and Hebrews scattered among the Christians, could the

18

conquest, even if that happened, be said to be complete ?

It is not surprising that the Inquisition had played no great part in medieval Spain, since the country had been only partly Christian, and the Christian kings had been confronted with the task of winning back the land from adversaries of another faith rather than with that of maintaining the integrity of their own. But, as we have already seen, Pedro II of Aragon had published a severe edict against heresy before the close of the twelfth century, and in 1226 James I forbade the entry of heretics into his kingdom. The latter fulmination was, doubtless, due to the natural tendency of persecuted Cathari of Languedoc to seek refuge across the Pyrenees in the nearest possible asylum, and it is because of the proximity of the heretics of the southeast of France that Aragon was troubled with the problem of heresy and that Castile was not.

In 1232 Gregory IX issued a bull, *Declinante*, to the Archbishop of Tarragona, ordering him to search out and punish all heretics within his diocese. It is of interest to note that this bull seems to have been issued under the influence

of a Spaniard, Raymond of Peñaforte, the
greatest Dominican of his day, who was
at this time very powerful at the papal
court and was perhaps the chief inspirer
of Gregory's policy of persecution and
therefore the original begetter of the
medieval Inquisition. The following year
James, on the advice of ecclesiastics assembled at Tarragona, promulgated a law
condemning landlords who protected heretics to forfeiture of their goods and declaring that anyone suspect of heresy was
incapable of holding office in the State.
In the year 1237 we find Dominican friars
active in tracking down heretics in the
kingdom ; next year they were assisted
by Franciscans. But persecution does not
appear to have been very effective, and in
1254 the King urged Pope Innocent IV
to make fresh efforts. The latter entrusted the search of heretics solely to
Dominicans. Exhortations of a council
which met at Tarragona in 1291 suggest
that the measures then being taken were,
at any rate in the eyes of the clergy,
inadequate. But ten years later the Inquisition was certainly vigorous, for we
hear of a number of burnings of obstinate
heretics, and several inquisitors of the
following period, notably Nicolas Roselli,

afterwards a cardinal, gained a great reputation from their energy.

The most remarkable of the medieval inquisitors of Spain was Nicolas Eymeric, whose *Directorium Inquisitorum* is the fullest, the most systematic and authoritative of all such manuals. Eymeric had a chequered career, for he fell under the displeasure of John I and twice had to go into exile. The King's hostility was due to the fact that Eymeric was the arch-enemy of the followers of Ramon Lull, one of the most extraordinary figures in the later Middle Ages, because of his erudition, the copiousness of his writing and the almost fanatical zeal with which he devoted his life to the attempt to convert the heretic and the infidel. Eymeric, whose *Directorium* is full of animus against him, considered that Lull had himself been a heretic, and in that work he enumerated no fewer than a hundred major errors of which he held him to be guilty. Lull's most heinous crimes in Eymeric's eyes were his trust in the efficacy of argument, of the appeal to the reason as a means of conversion, and his contention that it was wrong to kill heretics and that Jews and Mohammedans could be saved. Lull had been a tertiary of the Franciscan order, and the extravagant admiration felt by many of the Minorites for the philosopher's memory aroused the utmost indignation in Eymeric, who was himself a Dominican. Well might the soul of Eymeric grow bitter, when the monarch himself was a friend of men whom he regarded as most dangerous heretics. Bitter too are Eymeric's complaints of the lack of funds from which the Aragonese tribunal suffered. Since the Inquisition's revenue was largely derived from confiscated property, this may mean either that the heretics of Aragon were few or that they were poor; perhaps it means both. Yet we are told that Eymeric's successor was very successful—that is to say, that he punished many heretics. In the middle of the fifteenth century there appear to have been a considerable number of Waldensians in the country, most of whom were reconciled, though a few were burnt. Early in the century a separate tribunal was established in Valencia; one had been instituted in the Balearic Islands nearly a hundred years before. But the multiplication of tribunals did not betoken an increase of power and the Holy Office in the kingdom does not seem to have exercised a great deal of influence or to have met with much respect in the fifteenth century.

While the Inquisition was weak in the kingdom of Aragon and its dependencies, in Castile it did not exist at all. Legend attributes the creation of a Castilian Inquisition to St. Dominic. It is natural enough to ascribe the origin of an institution with which his followers were so closely connected to a great organizer and preacher who was a fervent missionary among heretics, but there was no Inquisition at all in Dominic's day. The truth is that Castile, unlike Aragon, had had no previous experience of the working of the Holy Office when Ferdinand and Isabella founded the modern Inquisition of Spain. But no part of the country had met with any tribunal so efficient or so powerful as this new institution to which the Catholic monarchs imparted not a little of their own characteristics—the masterfulness of the one, the religious zeal of the other. The inauguration of the new Inquisition by the Catholic monarchs must be regarded as an integral part of their policy of political organization and unification. It was rendered possible by the advance which the process of unifica-

tion had already made ; it was the result
of the gradual Christian reconquest of
the Peninsula ; it may indeed be regarded
as inaugurating the final stage in that
process.

CHAPTER II

AMONG many people Spain passes as a byword for religious intolerance, but its history in the earlier Middle Ages at all events most signally falsifies this reputation, since it was remarkable among the countries of Europe for the comparative amity and the freedom of social and commercial intercourse which existed between Christians, Jews and Muslims. In the twelfth and thirteenth centuries the Christians, under the inspiration of such leaders as Alfonso VI, Alfonso X and Archbishop Raimundo of Toledo, were keen to assimilate the Moorish culture graced by an Avempace, the Jewish culture which boasted a Maimonides. Even when the Christian reconquest began, the conquered Moors were permitted to remain in possession of their property and to practise their religion freely. They and the Jews formed a most valuable section of the community. They supplied the public services, the professions and the industries of the country with their most efficient and indefatigable workers. Valencia owed its prosperity, not only to the natural fertility of its soil, but also to the willing and trustworthy labour of its predominantly Moorish inhabitants in its orange groves, its olive terraces, its plantations of fig and date. In many parts of the country, in the rural districts and also in the towns, the application and enterprise of the adherents of these alien religions stood in marked contrast to the indolence of the native race. The Jews were particularly useful to the Christian kingdoms during the wars against the Moors because of their money and their financial skill, of which the sovereigns fully availed themselves.

But from the beginning of the fourteenth century there was a marked deterioration in the position of the non-Christian peoples in the Peninsula. There had been a foretaste of a more fanatical attitude just after the battle of Las Navas de Tolosa, when, at the instigation of the Archbishops of Toledo and Narbonne, there was a great slaughter of Moors gathered in Ubeda. Clerical influence was opposed to the free intercourse of Christian and non-Christian peoples, and it was effective in bringing about a very different state of affairs in the fourteenth century. The Jews were at no time popular. The same qualities which commended them to the ruler made them odious to his subjects. They were expert money-lenders as well as efficient tax-collectors. Although usury was indispensable for the maintenance of trade and the progress of industry, Christian moralists united in condemning it as sinful, and thus debtors, reluctant to pay what they owed, had the satisfaction of knowing on the highest canonical authority that their creditors were malefactors. Moreover, the Jews were an easy mark for envy because their love of display found vent in a lavish indulgence in splendour. Insensate hatred of the Jews was more slowly aroused in Spain than in other countries, and attempts on the part of more than one pope to induce Spanish rulers to force their non-Christian subjects to wear some distinctive garb, in order to prevent intermarriage, were abortive. In Castile especially the Jews received adequate

27   c

protection from the Crown up to the accession of the House of Trastamara.

Ere this a growing spirit of intolerance had been exemplified by two ecclesiastical councils, those of Zamora (1313) and Valladolid (1322), which issued canons intended to restrict as far as possible the intercourse of Christians with Moors and Jews. The frequent preference shown to Jews over Christians in appointments to political offices was denounced; as also the practice of employing Moors and Jews as physicians. Later on in the century the attempt was made to enforce the segregation of these alien peoples by restricting them to special quarters in the towns known respectively as *morerias* and *juderias*, it being ordered that these districts should be surrounded each by a wall having one entrance only. The people were incited against the Jews in particular by the eloquence of preachers whose zeal was due to perfectly sincere motives, since they were convinced that intercourse between the Christians and the Jews would lead to the contamination of the Christian faith. There were massacres of Jews in Castile, Aragon and Navarre, the most serious breaking out in Seville in 1391 directly as the result

28

of the perfervid zeal against the Hebrews of an archdeacon named Martínez, and spreading to Córdova and Toledo, to Burgos and other Castilian towns. There were similar outrages in the same year in the cities of Aragon and in Majorca.

The massacres of 1391 are an important turning-point in the history of the Jews in Spain. The favoured position which they had enjoyed in contrast to their lot in other countries was brought to an end, and the only way in which they could hope to retain their economic position with any security was by the acceptance of Christian baptism. Wholesale conversions undoubtedly followed the massacres of 1391. Llorente, whose figures are always rather imaginative, puts the figure as high as a million; they may not have been as numerous as a fifth or even a tenth of that number, but it is certain that very many Jews entered the Christian Church before the end of 1391, and that the process of conversion went on rapidly after that, being aided by the tremendous efforts in proselytism of St. Vicente Ferrer. Judaism was not entirely blotted out; indeed it raised its head once again before the final catastrophe; but it never really recovered from the disaster of 1391. From our point of view the importance of that year lies in the creation of a new community of Christianized Jews, Conversos or Marranos as they sometimes were called. They speedily became a very numerous, wealthy and influential section of the population. The gifts and characteristics of their race did not desert them, while their position was no longer prejudiced by the odium attached to Judaism. But the Conversos were not nearly as strongly entrenched as at first sight it would appear. A Jewish tax-gatherer or money-lender did not become any more popular because he was a Christianized Jew; indeed he might become even less so. There were plenty of people only too ready to believe that he had simply freed himself from the disabilities of Judaism by an entirely insincere profession of Christianity. Conversions inspired by the fear of massacre are not likely to be more than skin-deep, and it is not surprising if many of the Jewish Conversos cherished hatred and not love for their new co-religionists. The mutual hostility between the races was but whetted by the enforced conversions. Old and New Christians fought one another savagely in Toledo and Ciudad

Real; in March 1473 the mob rose in Córdova and attacked Jews and Conversos indiscriminately.

To the enforced conversion of Jews succeeded the enforced conversion of Moors. It was but natural that Ferdinand and Isabella should aspire to conquer the last remnant of independent Muslim Spain. The subjugation of the kingdom of Granada proved to be a formidable undertaking involving nine years of difficult fighting, from 1483 to 1492. As is often the case when the work of conquest has been arduous, very favourable terms were allowed to the conquered, and when in November 1491 the city of Granada itself was captured, a solemn engagement was entered into binding Ferdinand and Isabella and their successors to protect the properties, social customs and religious practices of the inhabitants. When an archbishopric of Granada was created it was conferred upon Hernando de Talavera, the Bishop of Avila and the Queen's confessor, a man of great benignity and enlightenment, who, though keenly desirous to win over the Mudéjares to Christianity, had no desire for unwilling proselytes. He himself learnt Arabic and made his assistant missionaries do the same; he won the confidence and affection of the Moors, and his efforts were remarkably successful.

They were not, however, phenomenal, and the process of conversion did not advance with sufficient rapidity to satisfy the two monarchs or the Archbishop of Toledo, Francisco Ximenes de Cisneros, whose name is one of the most illustrious in Spanish history. A man of the highest character and of very great learning, he was possessed of an imperious will and volcanic energy. Under his inspiration the forcible conversion of the Moors was undertaken despite the guarantees which had been given them and the tumultuous outbreaks which it provoked. When the process had made sufficient headway, an order was issued (July 1501) forbidding the Moors of other parts of Spain to enter the province of Granada, in order to secure the New Christians there from contamination. Next year followed a more drastic edict, whose preamble declared that since the kingdom of Granada had been practically cleansed of the infidel, it would be scandalous to allow Muslims to continue to live in other parts of Spain. All Muslims in Castile and Leon were therefore ordered to quit that kingdom before the ensuing April save in the case of boys under fourteen and girls under twelve. As they were forbidden to enter Aragon or Navarre or to join their co-religionists in northern Africa, this edict of 1502 rendered the prescribed emigration very difficult of execution, and it was therefore in effect if not in intention an edict of forcible conversion.

In Aragon, where the powers possessed by the Cortes provided checks upon the royal authority for which there was no counterpart in Castile, the lead given by Isabella's edict of 1502 was not followed and Ferdinand had to pledge himself not to attempt conversion of the Muslim population by force. Ferdinand's promise secured the Moorish people of Aragon in the enjoyment of their religion during the remainder of his lifetime; but when the social war, known as the *Germania*, broke out between commons and nobles in 1520 on the accession of the Emperor Charles V (Charles I of Spain), the former perpetrated many massacres of Moors, who as a rule loyally supported their masters, or forced baptism upon them. Finally, in November 1525, Charles issued an edict decreeing the banishment of all the Mohammedans of Aragon, Catalonia and Valencia. As in 1502, so in 1525, such restrictions were placed upon the exodus that the edict produced very many at least nominal conversions.

The conquest of Granada indirectly affected those Jews in Spain who had held fast to their faith despite the apprehensions naturally aroused by the catastrophe of 1391. So long as the threat of a separate Muslim State in the country remained the financial assistance of the Jews had been too valuable to be dispensed with ; but now fast upon the decision to banish the Mohammedans followed the decision to banish the Jews. Torquemada, soon to become famous as the first Inquisitor-general, incessantly urged upon Isabella the duty of ridding her lands of the polluting presence of the crucifiers of Christ. The story is familiar of how when the rumour spread that the expulsion of their race had been decided upon, Dr. Isaac Albravenal and another wealthy Jew offered 300,000 ducats in the hope of preventing this. Ferdinand was in favour of acceptance, when Torquemada suddenly appeared before the two sovereigns holding a crucifix before him and crying, " Behold the Crucified whom the wicked Judas sold for thirty pieces of silver ! If you approve the deed, sell Him for a greater sum." On March 30, 1492, the edict was issued which allowed the Jews just four months to decide whether to leave the country or to change their religion. Popular passion was aroused against the unfortunate race by the recital of the outrages, the murders, the insults to the Cross of which they were alleged to have been guilty during past centuries, and they were accused of inciting the Conversos to apostacy. Contemporary authorities put the number of the Jews who were exiled from Spain in consequence of this edict as high as half a million or considerably more. The historian Mariana suggests 800,000. Perhaps as many as 200,000 went into banishment, and as many as 50,000 purchased immunity by paying the price of baptism. Bernáldez puts the latter figure at 70,000, adding that " in the city of Granada there remained no one to baptize."

" Always using religion as a plea," says Machiavelli, Ferdinand " devoted himself with a pious cruelty to driving out and clearing the kingdom of the Marranos." The aim and object of Ferdinand's cold-blooded policy was undoubtedly the realization of national uniformity in the interests of statecraft, but in carrying it out he owed much to the assistance of those who were actuated by motives, not of expediency, but of piety, and who unfeignedly believed that the purity of the Christian religion in Spain was in imminent danger owing to the corrupting influence of many thousands of Jews and Mohammedans. The Jews and Mohammedans were driven out, but in their place there was a large population of potential heretics, of people nurtured in the faith and traditions of Moses or Islam, who had in the great majority of cases reluctantly accepted Christianity simply in order to escape death or banishment, who in the nature of the case had no reason to love or venerate the religion actually or virtually enforced upon them, and who for the most part received so little instruction in its principles and its doctrines that they were peculiarly liable to deviate from its creed and ritual. When it is remembered, moreover, that these new members of the Christian Church, especially the Jewish Conversos, were the objects very often of suspicion, jealousy and abhorrence, it will be realized that they ran very serious risk of falling into the hands of a tribunal created to maintain the unsullied purity of the faith.

That the Christianity of many of the Conversos was the merest veneer is undoubtedly true. The religion of their ancestors was in their blood ; it was not something which could be cast off as a matter of will ; they continued to practise in secret the rites to which they had been accustomed and paid to Christianity only the lip-service and outward semblance which safety required. Some indeed seem to have imagined that a nominal conformity would suffice and took fewer precautions for concealment than was prudent. They grossly miscalculated the situation. The Church was resolute not to permit the carrying on of Judaic or Muslim practices under a thin disguise of Christianity by persons who, whatever their motives in accepting it, had received baptism. The fathers at the great Council of Basel having drawn the attention of bishops to the need of watchfulness for the detection of hypocritical converts, John II of Castile in 1451 asked Nicholas V to delegate inquisitorial powers to a representative in his kingdom to deal with this problem ; whereupon the Pope entrusted the desired powers to his vicar-general, the Bishop of Osma. The arm of so weak a prince as John II could afford but little support to this attempt and it is probable that not much was accomplished. A few years later a learned friar named Alonso de Espina, himself a New Christian, delivered a fanatical onslaught upon the Jews and Conversos in ·a work entitled *Fortalicium Fidei*, in which were raked together all the old credulous tales (of which that of St. Hugh of Lincoln is a sample) of the murdering of children and poisoning of wells by the Jews. When Antichrist should come the Hebrew race would be found in league with him. As an elementary measure of security, their forcible conversion should be carried on wholesale, and for the safeguarding of the Church in Spain the lapses of the Conversos should be severely dealt with by an efficient Inquisition. In 1478 appeared the *Historia de los Reyes Catolicos*, of Andrés Bernáldez, the curate of Los Palacios, who in his chronicle utters a savage diatribe against the accursed race of the Jews. Judaism, according to him, had at the time of the accession of the Catholic sovereigns spread even among church dignitaries—for many of Jewish descent had risen to places of dignity in Church as well as in State—and they were teaching

the law of Moses rather than that of
Christ. Nominal converts were refraining
from having their children baptized, or
when they could not avoid that ceremony
were washing off the water of the chrism
afterwards; they observed the Jewish
Sabbath, the Passover and other Jewish
festivals; they ate meat in Lent and on
the other fast days of the Christian
Church.

There can be no doubt of the truth of
these allegations, which are substantiated
by the evidence of one inquisitorial process
after another, and if the outbursts of de
Espina and Bernáldez seem extravagant
and preposterous to modern ears, we must
remember that the really significant thing
about them is that the wildness of their
language is an indication of the sincerity
and intensity of their authors' apprehensions. The latter were in a genuine not a
feigned panic, fearful lest Christianity in
Spain should be destroyed by the Conversos who were rather converting Christians to Judaism than showing themselves
real converts to Christianity. People who
allow themselves to be panic-stricken are
not likely to discern facts clearly and in
their proper perspective, and no doubt
those who saw in the existence of insincere

39

Conversos a formidable menace to the Catholic Church in Spain greatly exaggerated the danger. Powers that were strong enough to enforce involuntary conversion upon people of an alien religion were strong enough to preserve their own. But we should not doubt the reality of the panic or dismiss its expression as mere fanaticism.

What it was that finally decided the Catholic sovereigns to establish a really effective Inquisition in their dominions is not known. The step was indeed the logical corollary of their pre-existing policy. In order to enforce law and order in a country where the ordinary machinery of central justice had broken down, they had instituted the sort of special police association known as the Santa Hermandad, which by summary and ruthless methods put down anarchy and punished crime with which the ordinary courts had proved themselves incompetent to deal. What was the institution of the Inquisition but the application to the ecclesiastical sphere of the same sort of system ? The ordinary episcopal courts had proved unable of themselves to maintain law and order and to preserve the faith from doctrinal anarchy ; they must therefore

40

be supplemented by courts possessed of a more efficient procedure and practising more drastic measures.

There is no question that Isabella's motive in furthering the Inquisition was sincere piety. Llorente attributes Ferdinand's decision to a desire to have a pretext for seizing the property of the Jews, always the wealthiest members of the community. Cupidity may have contributed to his zeal, but fundamentally he was inspired by the determination, shared by all the powerful monarchs of his time, whether Catholic or Protestant, to maintain order, uniformity and obedience to authority in Church as well as in State. There had been much prompting by eminent ecclesiastics, such notably as Archbishop Mendoza of Toledo and Torquemada. Ludovico à Paramo, the Sicilian inquisitor, in his work on the origin of the Holy Inquisition, tells us that the decisive event was the discovery that the Jews and Conversos had deliberately planned a great clandestine Judaic celebration for the night of Good Friday 1478. However that may be, it was in the year 1478 that the Catholic sovereigns requested Sixtus IV that an Inquisition might be established in Castile. The papal bull authorizing this, dated November, merely notes the existence of many false Christians in Spain and empowers Ferdinand and Isabella in consequence to appoint three bishops or other fitting persons, being priests and at least forty years of age, learned either in theology or in the common law, to have jurisdiction over heresy within the kingdom of Castile. There was an interval of two years before the bull was put into execution; but on September 17, 1480, two Dominican friars were appointed to act as inquisitors in Seville.[1] They were subsequently given the assistance of a promotor-fiscal or prosecutor and of two receivers of confiscations.

Arrived upon the scene of their labours, the two inquisitors called upon all the nobles of the neighbourhood to deliver to them all persons suspect of heresy and to sequestrate their property. Soon finding their original quarters too small for them, they removed to the great fortress of Triana on the outskirts of the city.

[1] H. del Pulgar, *Cronica de los Reyes Catolicos* (Valencia, 1780), p. 136; D. Ortiz de Zuñiga, *Anales Eclesiasticos . . . de Sevilla* (Madrid, 1677), p. 386; Ludovico à Paramo, *De Origine et Progressu Sanctae Inquisitionis* (Madrid, 1598), p. 130.

Some of the most prominent Conversos of Seville and the surrounding district plotted to slay the inquisitors in the hope of administering so thorough a fright that the idea of establishing a tribunal in their midst would be abandoned. But the conspiracy was betrayed, and many of the most influential Conversos of the city were arrested on the charge of complicity in it. On February 6, 1481, the first public ceremony, or *auto de fe*, of the newly established Inquisition was held and six persons were burnt at the stake. Other victims followed a few days later. Terrified by these events, a number of Conversos sought safety in flight. The plot, instead of embarrassing, had helped the new Inquisition. The original tribunal at Seville was speedily supple- mented by others—in Córdova, Jaen, Ciudad Real, the last-mentioned being afterwards transferred to Toledo.

Apart from the abortive plot just re- ferred to, the tribunals in Castile seem to have met with but little opposition and indeed to have been welcomed by the majority of the inhabitants. It was otherwise when Ferdinand decided to substitute for the now moribund papal Inquisition in Aragon one on the new

Castilian model. When he essayed to do this he met with obstinate resistance from the Pope, who had already realized that the new type of Inquisition in Spain was much more under royal than under papal control. But eventually after a prolonged controversy Sixtus IV gave way and Torquemada became inquisitor in Aragon as he already was in Castile. Permanent tribunals were established in the cities of Saragossa, Barcelona and Valencia. There was trouble in each province of the Aragonese kingdom. The Cortes of Valencia protested against the new Inquisition as a violation of their *fueros*, or liberties ; the officials refrained from giving assistance to the inquisitors ; the nobles put obstacles in their path by sheltering fugitives until Ferdinand ordered them under penalty of a heavy fine to surrender such persons to the inquisitors' officer, or *alguazil*. Catalonia had always been particularly jealous of its liberties, and it objected to being brought under the jurisdiction of Torquemada. As a matter of fact, Barcelona already had inquisitors of its own, Dominican friars who continued to act under the old papal dispensation. Ferdinand was determined to be rid of them, and eventually Innocent VIII, under the excuse that they had been over-officious, consented, and Torquemada's nominees took their place. Although the area for which the Barcelona tribunal was responsible was very extensive, stretching from Tarragona as far north as Perpignan, it dealt with relatively few cases in its early years ; which probably indicates that it continued to meet with inadequate local support.

It was in Aragon itself that the most serious difficulties were encountered. Here the Marranos were particularly influential, not only by reason of their wealth, but because many of them were connected by marriage with noble houses. The first two inquisitors in Saragossa were a friar named Gaspar Juglar and a canon of the cathedral, Pedro Arbués d'Epila. Their initial proceedings were carried through without hindrance, and they celebrated *autos de fe* in May and June 1484 at which a number of New Christians were burnt as Judaizers. But it was not long before they found that their activities were being impeded by a lack of whole-hearted support on the part of the officials and lawyers, a good many of whom were themselves Conversos. Active resistance came first from the city

45

of Teruel, where it had been decided to found another tribunal. The officials of this place, obviously with popular concurrence, refused to admit the inquisitors within their gates. Ferdinand, who was very angry, stopped the salaries of all the magistrates of Teruel and evidently contemplated much more drastic action, but it is not clear whether this was needed.

Meanwhile, some of the most notable Conversos of Saragossa were plotting to rid themselves of the obnoxious tribunal within their city, but they were so dilatory in their proceedings that Ferdinand had warning that a conspiracy was on foot long before the ringleaders carried out their plans and murdered Arbués as he knelt near the high altar in Saragossa Cathedral. The deed was as foolish and shortsighted as it was criminal. The signal for the Albigensian Crusades had been the slaying of a priest named Pierre de Castelnau. History repeated itself. Like Pierre de Castelnau, Arbués was looked upon as a martyr and a pious hatred of the heretic was engendered such as had not existed before. The Old Christians were infuriated and in their execration of the criminals gave enthusiastic support to the inquisitors. The city mob furiously demanded the blood of the murderous and sacrilegious Marranos. Weapons which the assassins had used were hung up in the cathedral in token of public humiliation. One by one those that had been implicated in the plot, even in the slightest measure, were brought to retribution, the flimsiest evidence being accepted. Scarcely a noble family in Aragon but saw one or other of its members disgraced at an *auto de fe*. Of the original unpopularity of the Inquisition in Aragon there can be no question ; it is attested even by Bernáldez. Nothing could have cleared its path more effectively than the stupendous blunder of the Conversos of Saragossa. As the chronicler Zurita puts it, " Under Providence the conspirators in trying to injure the Inquisition greatly assisted it." [1]

Opposition to the Inquisition and its methods was, however, by no means ended by the murder of Arbués. The Cortes of the three component divisions of the kingdom of Aragon were jealous of any infringement of their *fueros*, and

[1] See G. Zurita, *Anales de la Corona de Aragon* (Madrid and Barcelona, 1853), Vol. V, pp. 657-62 ; G. de Castellano y de la Peña, *Un Complot terrorista en el Siglo XV* (Madrid, 1927).

were quick to challenge the tendency which soon became apparent for inquisitors to extend their jurisdiction. In 1512 representatives of Aragon, Catalonia and Valencia meeting together at Monzon drew up statements of grievances of very similar content. They complained of the extravagant multiplication of inquisitorial officials, of claims put forward to exemption from local taxation as well as of demands that the trial of cases of usury, bigamy, sorcery in addition to those of heresy should be undertaken by the new tribunals. As the result of these representations an agreement or *concordia* was come to between the King, the Inquisitor-general and the Cortes by which the jurisdiction of the tribunals was to be restricted to actual heresy and to crimes in which heresy was implied.

On the accession of Charles V these agreements were confirmed. The new ruler was not at first disposed to favour the Inquisition, being under the influence of Chièvres and other Flemish advisers, who had little sympathy with Spain institutions. But reiterated complaints of the Aragonese Cortes indicate that the *concordias* were not operative and that other promises made by Charles were not effective. Among these promises were that those who gave information to the inquisitors should be closely examined as to their motives ; that prisoners should have access to their kith and kin ; that the accused should be informed of the names of those who had given evidence against him ; that children should not be deprived of their property because their parents had been found guilty of heresy. It is clear that the chief reason why it was in Aragon, which had had previous experience of the working of an inquisition, and not in Castile, which had none, that complaints against the new tribunals were loudest and most sustained. is that there was so striking a contrast between the methods of the old Inquisition, which had become too debilitated to insist upon complete confiscation, and the new Inquisition, which exacted it to the uttermost farthing and thereby impoverished many innocent persons together with the guilty.

There was much less popular criticism of the conduct of the Inquisition in Castile except when there was patent misconduct, as in the case of an inquisitor of Córdova, Lucero by name, who at the opening of the sixteenth century displayed almost maniacal zeal in the discharge of his duties. He was convinced that there existed a great conspiracy to substitute Judaism for Christianity throughout Spain. His investigations into this apocryphal plot led to so many arrests that a reign of terror was created, particularly as Lucero accused persons of unblemished reputation and rigid orthodoxy, even imputing Judaism to the venerable Talavera, Archbishop of Granada. Lucero's misguided zeal led to such outrageous results that after a lengthy trial he was dismissed from his office. Other abuses were discovered about the same time, and Ximenes, who was Inquisitor-general in Castile from 1507 to 1517, dismissed a number of unsatisfactory inquisitors. Otherwise occasional complaints made by the Castilian Cortes and many attempts made by the Conversos to induce Charles V to mitigate the severity of the Inquisition were quite fruitless. It was not long before that monarch became as fully convinced as Ferdinand had ever been of the great utility of the tribunals, while his religious convictions were as sincere as they were bigoted, which cannot be said of Ferdinand. During his reign the Inquisition was more firmly fastened than ever upon every part of Spain, and in his last days he charged Philip II, his successor, to support the Holy Office to the uttermost.

CHAPTER III

ORGANIZATION, POWERS AND PRIVILEGES
OF THE INQUISITION

THE Spanish Inquisition in its great days before decay set in was undoubtedly efficient for its purpose. Its potency was due to royal support and to good organization. Ferdinand and Isabella were successful rulers largely because they achieved centralization of administration in the hands of four great Councils, the Council of State, the Council of Finance, the Council of Castile, the Council of Aragon. To these, with the assent of Sixtus IV, they added a fifth—the Council of the Inquisition or the Suprema. The Pope was ready to agree to the setting up of this body because it testified to the great importance attached to matters of faith by the Spanish sovereigns, but he thereby unsuspectingly sanctioned a very real limitation of papal authority, since the activities of the various tribunals were co-ordinated by a national authority, not by Rome. Central control was also exercised through the office of Inquisitor-general, first occupied by Torquemada, who had several particularly notable successors—Diego Deza, Ximenes, Adrian of Utrecht (afterwards Pope Adrian VI), Alfonso Manrique, Fernando Valdés. For a short period—from 1507 to 1518—the Inquisitions of Castile and Aragon were separated, and there were two Inquisitors-general. Except for that short period one Inquisitor-general supervised all the tribunals in Spain and its dependencies. The relations between him and the Suprema were not clearly defined and depended largely upon his personality. Torquemada was a despot, who often acted without taking the Council into his confidence. Thus, the very important regulations which he drew up in 1484, 1488 and 1498, known as the *Instrucciónes Antiguas*, upon which the procedure of the Spanish tribunal was based, were issued on his own authority. But after his death the Suprema became more powerful, and when, owing to the necessity of framing new rules to fit types of cases which had arisen since the issue of the first code, the masterful Valdés issued in 1561 the *Instrucciónes Nuevas*, it was expressly stated that they had been discussed in the

Council. But the days of autocrats were not over, and Diego Arce y Reynoso, who was Inquisitor-general from 1643 to 1665, was almost as dictatorial as Torquemada. From the commencement of the seventeenth century the Inquisitor-general was *ex-officio* president of the Suprema, but this had not been the custom before. At one time the president actually enjoyed the larger salary. If the latter was a strong and ambitious man there was very apt to be friction between the two potentates.

The most serious clash between the Inquisitor-general and the Council arose in the reign of the miserable Charles II, whose life of forty years was a continual torment, while all the chancellories of Europe waited expectant of his anticipated early demise. The sufferings of the King were attributed to his having been bewitched by a certain demoniacally possessed nun, who enjoyed the favour of a member of the Suprema named Froilan Díaz. The question whether the ecstatic utterances of the nuns ought to be taken seriously—and they were taken very seriously indeed by one of the rival parties at Court—became a matter of first-rate political importance. Mendoza y Sandoval, the Inquisitor-general, regarded Froilan Díaz as suspect of heresy and made arrangements for his trial. The Suprema came to the conclusion that there was no case and voted for the suspension of the process, which was equivalent to acquittal. Mendoza then brought the matter before the tribunal at Murcia, and, that also failing him, before the tribunal at Madrid. He had the satisfaction of keeping Díaz for four years in confinement pending a decision at Madrid. Meanwhile Charles II died, being succeeded in 1701 by Philip of Bourbon, who brought new methods as well as a new dynasty into Spain. Mendoza, who had supported the Austrian claimant to the throne, was now out of favour. Contrary to all the traditions of the Spanish Inquisition, Mendoza referred the matter in dispute to the Papacy, and declared that the members of the Suprema in claiming to have a deciding as well as a consultative voice were guilty of error and heresy. Finally Philip restored to the Council three of its members whom Mendoza had disgraced. Froilan Díaz was subsequently also restored, and in 1705 Mendoza had to resign his position as Inquisitor-general.

The tendency, then, was for the Suprema

to increase its authority, and it became in the sixteenth and seventeenth centuries a very powerful oligarchy. Its influence naturally expanded as it succeeded in making its control over the local tribunals more and more effective, this process being furthered by improving means of communication and by the selection by Philip II of Madrid as a permanent capital for the whole of Spain. Thus the independence of action which had been shown by the tribunals in the early days of the Inquisition was more and more curtailed, and the Suprema intervened in a remarkably large proportion of the trials. In 1647 it ordered that all sentences passed were to be immediately submitted for its approval. Such centralization was undoubtedly salutary. It ensured uniformity of practice, whereas hitherto in spite of the *Instrucciónes* there had been considerable divergence between the methods of one tribunal and another. It also promoted leniency, since local inquisitors were brought to book for any extravagances or undue severity of which they had been guilty. Originally the Council's principal function had been its appellate jurisdiction, but as it came to intervene more and more in the initial proceedings undertaken by

56

the tribunals, appeals became fewer and mattered less.

The Suprema also had a great deal of financial business to transact, and it was largely due to its holding the funds of the Inquisition that its control over the tribunals was so powerful. All current income derived from fines and confiscations had to be handed over to the Council, which paid all salaries; contributions which had to be made to the royal exchequer were paid in by the Council; all investments held by the tribunals were held in the name of the Council. From the sums paid in by the tribunals, including those in the Colonies, the Suprema accumulated a large capital, while great sums of money, both in revenue and expenditure, necessarily passed through its hands.

Behind the Inquisitor-general and the Council of the Inquisition stood the Spanish monarchy and the Papacy. Ferdinand was the true creator of the modern Spanish Inquisition; it was he who gave it its distinctively national character. The masterful creator was bound to have power over the thing which he had created. He was ever zealous for its influence and authority, but this was largely because he regarded it as a great asset of the Crown.

He would have none but persons agreeable to himself appointed as inquisitors; he would permit no inquisitor to receive a papal bull without communicating its contents to him. It is not true that he applied the institution to secular purposes, and he did not interfere with its main activities, where matters of doctrine were concerned. On the other hand, he was convinced that the success of its legitimate operations was of first-rate importance to the monarchy, and he was anxious that its business should be efficiently conducted. He therefore paid close personal attention to its finances, but Lea, who examined the evidence carefully, formed a very favourable opinion of Ferdinand's conduct in such matters, finding that he often reached decisions adverse to himself and gave evidence of " an innate sense of justice unexpected in a monarch who ranked next to Cæsar Borgia in the estimation of Machiavelli." [1]

Ferdinand often communicated directly with the tribunals; his successors dealt only with the Inquisitor-general and the Suprema, leaving to them the appoint-

[1] *History of the Inquisition of Spain* (4 vols., 1922), Vol. I, p. 297. Cf. Zurita, *Anales de la Corona de Aragon*, p. 641.

ment of all subordinate officers. On the other hand, the King always selected the Inquisitor-general, though this right was never formally acknowledged by the Pope when making the appointment, and this assisted him in preserving the essentially national character of the Spanish Inquisition. While continuing to safeguard the Crown's control as against that of the Papacy, the Spanish monarchs after the reign of Philip II and before the accession of the Bourbons proved less able to dominate the Suprema. Royal control over the Inquisition's finances was much restricted, and accurate statements regarding the proceeds of fines and confiscations became virtually unobtainable. Jealous of its authority over the tribunals, the Council in 1562 gave instructions that if the Government made an inquiry directly of any one of them, the reply should be sent that the information desired would be sent through the Inquisitor-general or the Suprema.

The ultimate authority over the Inquisition as over all other ecclesiastical institutions was that of the Pope, but both the King and the Suprema did their best to avoid all external intervention as far as possible. Nevertheless, the Papacy was always a power to be reckoned with, and in its numerous disputes with the Spanish King and the Council, it was sometimes victorious, and if it gave way this was because a bargain had been struck from which it derived other advantage. Finding the authorities both civil and ecclesiastical in Spain to be adamant to their remonstrances, the Conversos often sought aid from Rome. They sometimes pleaded before the Inquisition their possession of a confessional letter, which was obtainable from the papal Penitentiary and which empowered any confessor selected by its holder to grant absolution from sins, including heresy. Such a system obviously stultified inquisitional action, and the Spanish Inquisition contended that it ought not to be used to prevent or to annul its proceedings. Sixtus IV at first insisted that those who had obtained this form of absolution must be protected, and then suspended the bull in which he had done so; Alexander VI would not allow the letters to be used in order to escape well-merited penalties; but Julius II and Leo X continued to issue them.

More important than the question of the validity of confessional letters was that of appeals to Rome from the decisions of the Inquisition. Wealthy Conversos frequently made such appeals, and not always in vain. Sometimes a pope was willing to delegate his appellate jurisdiction to the Inquisitor-general. Innocent VIII, Alexander VI, Leo X, Adrian VI and Clement VII all did so; but obviously the power which decided to delegate its authority might also decide to retain it. If those who sought protection from the Papacy could never be certain of obtaining it, neither could the Inquisition be sure that they would not obtain it.

Two of the most important cases which ever came before the Spanish Inquisition involved the question of its relation with the Curia—those of Archbishop Carranza and Geronimo de Villanueva, Marquis of Villalba.

The first of these created a stir throughout Catholic Europe, which was amazed to see the Archbishop of Toledo put upon his trial for heresy. Had the Inquisition the power to proceed against a bishop? The question, which had been answered very decidedly in the negative by Boniface VIII, had only an academic interest in the Middle Ages; but in sixteenth-century Spain, where Conversos sometimes reached the episcopate and Old Christians were apt to suspect the orthodoxy of any Converso, it became one of practical importance. In its early days the Spanish Inquisition did not attempt to try bishops, but Torquemada denounced two, both of Jewish birth, to Rome, and one, at any rate, of them was degraded. It was no doubt in consequence of the spread of Lutheranism in Europe that Clement VII gave to Manrique in 1531 the right of investigating the beliefs of any bishop suspected of harbouring Protestant opinions, but not of arresting or imprisoning him. Similarly in January 1559 Paul IV entrusted Valdés with this faculty of inquiry, in consultation with the Suprema, and added the right to imprison if there was reason to suppose that flight was contemplated.

Valdés utilized the later papal brief against Archbishop Carranza. The prosecution has been attributed to the personal malevolence of Valdés and of a noted Dominican, Melchor Cano, but it has to be admitted that Carranza, who was a man of exemplary life, and who, far from being a heretic by intent, prided himself upon the active part he had taken against the English heretics at the Court of Mary Tudor when he accompanied his master

Philip II to England, was not at all a clear thinker and very far from circumspect in utterance. The Archbishop enjoyed the friendship and esteem of Philip II ; his arrest and imprisonment was effected during the King's absence from the country. The rich revenues of the see of Toledo were sequestrated, passing into the royal possession. The process dragged on and on : the powers under which Valdés had originally taken action extended for only two years ; they were four times renewed. The interminable delays are attributed to Carranza himself by Bishop Simancas, whose treatise, *De Catholicis Institutionibus*, is one of our principal authorities on the Spanish Inquisition. It has been suggested with perhaps greater plausibility that they were due to the fact that if Philip had once liked Carranza, he now liked the Toledo revenues still more.

At all events the King had become the strong supporter of the cause of Valdés and the Suprema in their claims to deal with the case of Carranza, despite the protests of the fathers assembled at the Council of Trent and of Pius IV who repeatedly remonstrated against the prolongation of the proceedings. At last the Pope, losing patience, insisted under pain of anathema

and the deprivation of their dignities of all
concerned that the case should be transferred to Rome and Carranza delivered up
to the papal nuncio. These commands
were ignored, and at the death of Pius IV
in December 1565 the case which had
started in May 1559 was still dragging on.

Pius V, who succeeded, was a man of
more powerful personality. No pontiff
was ever a more fervent enemy of the heretic, but Pius was an equally determined
asserter of the rights of the Holy See.
Philip's ambassador in Rome reported that
the new pope was actuated by no consideration of private interest and thought
only of what was just, and the King was
to find him quite immovable. Pius demanded that Carranza should immediately
be sent to Rome. Philip spoke of the
demand as being contrary to the royal
prerogative. The Pope expressed his
indignation at such an answer ; he described the treatment of Carranza as a
scandal, deprived Valdés and the Suprema
of all jurisdiction in the case, and under
terrible threats of anathema and excommunication reiterated his orders. Philip
had to decide whether to risk a complete
rupture with the Papacy in defence of the
independence claimed by the Inquisition.

He was strongly urged by Valdés and the more bellicose members of the Suprema to stand firm, and he tried, in accordance with his usual policy, to procrastinate; but eventually he yielded before the Pope's displeasure, and Carranza was sent to Rome for papal judgment, which was not pronounced till nine years later, during the pontificate of Gregory XIII. The question of Carranza's guilt, which is not here in point, will be considered in connection with the story of Spanish Protestantism.[1]

Villanueva was Secretary of State for Aragon in the reign of Philip IV, whose favour to the Inquisition was almost abject. Like Froilan Díaz, he got into trouble because of his patronage of a convent where the nuns became demoniacally possessed, declaring in their transports that the convent would be the means of the regeneration of the Church. Realizing the possible danger he ran owing to the interest he had shown in the nuns' prophecies, Villanueva made a voluntary confession. The Suprema decided that there was no case against him and gave him a certificate to that effect. Eleven years later a charge of heresy was preferred

[1] See *infra*, pp. 143–6.

against him at the instance of personal enemies, and to his utter astonishment he found himself arrested and imprisoned. The case was eventually referred to the Suprema, which severely reprimanded him, ordered him to abjure, and banished him from the cities of Madrid and Toledo and their vicinity for three years.

The sentence was not in itself severe, but it meant the ruin of Villanueva's career, and, with the devoted help of many relatives and friends, he made vehement efforts to avoid these penalties. As the result of many representations the Pope, Innocent X, resolved to hear the case on appeal, and dispatched a brief instructing the Bishop of Calahorra or one of two other bishops to hear the case as his representative. The masterful Inquisitor-general, Arce y Reynoso, ordered the Bishop of Calahorra not to receive the brief. Innocent threatened to deprive the rebellious Inquisitor-general of his office, and a new brief was dispatched—this time to the Bishop of Avila. The King, who was completely under the influence of Arce in this matter, took the high-handed action of seizing the papal brief. Thus the Inquisition, aided and abetted by Philip, set the Pope at defiance. In 1650

Innocent decided that the case should be transferred to the Apostolic See and ordered that all the papers bearing upon it should be forwarded to Rome, under pain of heavy penalties for the Inquisitor-general and his assistants. When it became clear that the Pope's resolution could not be worn down by procrastination and the pronouncement was made that by their recalcitrance the Inquisitor-general and the Suprema had incurred the penalty of deprivation of their functions, Arce still counselled resistance, asserting that compliance would mean the undoing of the Inquisition ; but the King and his counsellors, less audacious, decided to yield and the papers relating to the trial of Villanueva were sent to Rome. Before a final decision could be reached the unfortunate man died ; and after that the Inquisition commenced an action against his memory, which Innocent's successor, Alexander VII, disallowed. From first to last the case occupied thirty-two years. Its chief interest and importance lies in the Inquisition's defiance of Rome. The Papacy was ultimately victorious over the rebels, in the case of Villanueva as in that of Carranza, but the prolonged and tenacious resistance made by the Inquisition in defence of its independence is hardly less significant. None other of the Inquisition's prisoners had the standing of Carranza ; few indeed had such influential and persistent friends as Villanueva. When the King, the Inquisitor-general and the Suprema were in accord, there was as a rule little prospect of success in appealing to Rome.

From a consideration of the directing powers of the Inquisition we may pass to the organization of the individual tribunals. In the early days the officials were few ; before long they became extremely numerous. In the year 1647 complaint was made in Palma that there were no fewer than 150 persons, exclusive of familiars, who were reckoned as functionaries of the Majorca tribunal. The less the Inquisition had to do, the greater became the number of its officials, and in the eighteenth century especially, when its great work was accomplished, there existed a large number of persons willing to accept a small pittance to which no real duties any longer attached, for the sake of the privileges and immunities which servants of the Inquisition enjoyed. In any case the duties of the smaller fry were light : hours were short, and penalties for slackness do not seem to have been severe or dismissals frequent. On the other hand, a fair level of efficiency was maintained by the occasional inspections of *visitadores*, who examined all officers, inquired into any neglect of regulations, scrutinized the records and went over the prisons.

The efficiency of each tribunal depended upon its principal officials, and most of all upon the inquisitors themselves, of whom there were normally two or three. The earliest inquisitors were, as we have seen, Dominican friars, and it was required that they should be learned either in theology or in law, and should be at least forty years old. The age was subsequently reduced to thirty, and it ceased for a time to be necessary that inquisitors should be in orders until in 1632 the Suprema, feeling that it was not seemly that laymen should be judges in heretical causes, reimposed this provision. The powers possessed by the inquisitors were very extensive, but latterly their independence of action was severely limited by the centralizing policy of the Suprema. Popular imagination has so distorted the picture of the ordinary inquisitor, representing him as an ogre possessed of a lust of cruelty, that it is perhaps desirable to say that, while there are certainly instances of inquisitors of unworthy character who abused a position of great responsibility, the large majority in all probability fulfilled the requirements that they should be " prudent and suitable men of good repute and sound conscience and zealous for the Catholic faith." If they were cruel it was from a sense of duty and not from wantonness.

Associated with the inquisitor was the bishop. Their relations were sometimes a little strained. It had been clearly understood in the medieval Inquisition that whenever torture was ordered and whenever the final sentence was pronounced episcopal concurrence was necessary, and Sixtus IV in 1482 drew attention to this ancient rule. But in Spain the bishop was not often present in person. He had many other duties to perform, and in the tribunal he was, despite his precedence, inferior in importance to the inquisitor, to whom he frequently delegated his authority. There might also be present a legal assessor, whose duty was to give advice on points of law to the inquisitors, whose training was much more often in theology than in jurisprudence. But at

70

no time was the assessor regarded as indispensable, and about the middle of the sixteenth century he disappears altogether.

Second only to the inquisitor in real importance came the promotor-fiscal or prosecutor. There was no such officer in the medieval Inquisition, where the procedure was strictly by *inquisitio* and not by *accusatio*. As time went on the status and consequence of the fiscal steadily improved. At first paid a much smaller salary as a subordinate of the inquisitor, he came to be regarded as almost if not quite his equal. Indeed, inquisitors were sometimes appointed to the office, and one finds the title inquisitor-fiscal in use.

The notaries or secretaries were a most essential cog in the inquisitorial machine. Their duties were to take detailed notes of interrogatories and other proceedings and to look after the records. In the earliest days of the Spanish Inquisition the notes were sometimes crude and fragmentary, and despite the constant exhortations of the Suprema the documents were not always very carefully preserved ; yet in process of time the Inquisition came to acquire a vast storehouse of information, including innumerable genealogical details, which were of inestimable value to it. All the families that had ever at any time been tainted with heresy came to be known, and the statements of a prisoner made before a tribunal in one part of the country could often be checked by the records of a tribunal at the other end of Spain.

Although they were paid no salary, the experts, known as *calificadores*, who were called upon to make a preliminary examination of the written evidence put in against the accused, or to examine his publications in the case of an author, were most important, since it was for them to decide whether there was a *prima facie* case to justify further action. They played an especially significant part in the trial of suspected Lutherans and of scholars whose orthodoxy was questioned, and when the censorship of books became one of the principal duties of the Inquisition *calificadores* were constantly needed for the examination of literature reputed to be heretical.

It will suffice simply to mention the minor functionaries of the tribunals—the *alguazil*, a sort of man of all works, whose chief business, however, was the arrest of prisoners and the seizing of their goods; the gaoler or *carcelero* ; the *portero*, who served notices and citations ; the physician, whose presence was required for the examination of prisoners before and after torture and for the investigation of cases of feigned or suspected madness ; the chaplain, who celebrated Mass for the inquisitors—not for the prisoners, who were denied the sacrament ; the barber ; and the receiver of confiscations, sometimes known as the treasurer.

In some tribunals additional officers existed, whom it is unnecessary to name ; but all tribunals had their familiars, who, with no well-defined duties, nevertheless bulk very largely in all accounts of the Inquisition, if only because complaints about them were so incessant. In the Middle Ages, when the inquisitor in the midst of a hostile population often went in danger of his life, he had customarily been protected by a bodyguard of armed men. In lieu of these permanent personal attendants the Spanish inquisitors were wont to appoint men all over the country who were prepared to give their services in return for the very substantial privileges which the Inquisition was able to bestow. The familiars came from every class in the community. The most illustrious grandees were happy to bear the standard of the Holy Office or to take some other part in the ceremonial of the *auto de fe*; humbler folk were prepared to act as spies or as guards or as simple hangers-on, as might be required of them. Familiars tended to become very numerous despite the efforts made by the Suprema from time to time to restrict their numbers, and they were often drawn from the most objectionable class of persons, who valued the privileges appertaining to the position precisely because their way of life rendered those immunities of practical advantages for evading the ordinary course of the law. An ambitious scheme was once propounded which would have placed at the disposal of the Holy Office a much more formidable force than that of the unorganized familiars. This was for forming a new military order to be known as that of *Santa Maria de la Espada Blanca*, with the Inquisitor-general as its head, to whom all the members were to swear implicit obedience. Philip II was a strong supporter of the Inquisition, but it is not surprising that he rejected a plan which would have created a semi-military oligarchy more powerful than the Orders of Sant Iago, Calatrava and Alcántara, which had in times past been so serious a menace to the Castilian monarchy.

It was to have been a necessary condition of membership of the projected order that the candidate should have in his veins no *mala sangre*, no taint of Jewish, Moorish, or heretical blood. This was a condition upon which the Inquisition eventually insisted for all those who served it in any capacity. The tendency for the Old Christians to look upon themselves as a caste apart, to take inordinate pride in their *limpieza*, or purity of blood, was not created by the Holy Office, and the military orders demanded it long before the Inquisition became so exacting. It was not until 1560 that the Suprema gave instructions that all familiars must be *limpios*. Henceforward applicants for even the most trivial unsalaried post had to show proof of *limpieza*. Where was such proof to be found ? The Inquisition itself possessed in its archives much the most voluminous evidence bearing upon this subject ; and indeed it soon became necessary for the aspirant not only to positions under the Holy Office but to practically every other post both in Church and State to apply to the Inquisition for the necessary proof. When such request was made the Inquisition was wont to make a charge before undertaking the necessary investigation, and the issuing of certificates of *limpieza* formed a useful new source of revenue. Inasmuch as even connection by marriage with a Jewish or Moorish family or the fact of having an ancestor who had been lightly penanced on suspicion of heresy involved *mala sangre*, quite a large proportion of Spaniards were not in a position to prove *limpieza*, and thus inevitably many men of fine ability and character were excluded from the public service of their country or their Church.

For those not debarred by *mala sangre* service under the Holy Office, especially if it was merely nominal, was naturally popular because of the great power wielded by the institution. Claiming autocratic authority, possessed of the spiritual weapons of anathema and excommunication, supported by the Crown in requiring of all secular officials an oath not only to aid it in its work but also to guard its immunities, the Inquisition could be as helpful to its friends as it was formidable to its foes.

It is difficult to generalize about the Inquisition's privileges. They varied from period to period; to some only salaried officials were entitled; some were universally recognized, others were sharply contested by the Cortes or by secular jurisdictions. Until the accession of the Bourbon dynasty at the opening of the eighteenth century, salaried officials usually enjoyed exemption from the payment of the national taxes. The claim of the familiars to this favour was never admitted, but they persistently pressed for it. Inquisitors from time to time endeavoured to secure exemption from the octroi and other local dues. In some places they were successful, but the assumption of this privilege gave rise to incessant disputes.

A number of other privileges may be briefly summarized—the right of inquisitors, when travelling about, to receive lodging free and food at special prices, and to exemption from the ordinary citizen's obligation to provide billets for soldiers. Another valued right was that of carrying arms, which was possessed by familiars as well as by regular functionaries of the Holy Office. This might be justified on the ground that the performance of certain duties, such as the arrest of influential offenders, sometimes involved danger; but it meant in practice that a large number of persons, including some of an irresponsible character, went about armed, to the advantage of none but themselves and sometimes to the detriment of the public welfare.

But the most precious of all privileges was that of freedom from the jurisdiction of other courts. The clergy were in any case outside the purview of secular justice, but what of the numerous lay hangers-on of the Inquisition ? It was claimed that suits in which an official of the Holy Office was involved, whether as defendant or as plaintiff, could be brought only before that tribunal. Both Ferdinand and Leo X laid it down that the right of exemption applied only to cases in which the official was a defendant, but while the King ruled that even this restricted privilege applied only to salaried officials, the Pope included familiars within its benefits. Charles V was at first willing to acquiesce in this immunity for familiars, but before long he changed his mind, having come to the conclusion that they were thereby induced to commit crimes which they would otherwise have been chary of doing. Finally, by a *concordia* or agreement of 1553 in Castile, it was stipulated that familiars should be subject to the secular tribunals in all civil cases and in all but minor criminal cases. There were particularly bitter complaints made in the kingdom of Aragon of the number of familiars and their frequent lawlessness, and in answer to representations made by the Cortes it was arranged that the multitude of familiars should be reduced to specified figures and that magistrates should be furnished with lists to facilitate the identification of persons entitled to privileges.

Despite the *concordias* in Castile and Aragon, friction between the Inquisition and other tribunals was not brought completely to an end. In its desire to protect its officers and servants the Holy Office was often in conflict, not only with secular, but also with other spiritual courts. Clashes between different systems of justice existing side by side in one country are a very common phenomenon, and the quarrels between the Spanish Inquisition and other jurisdictions are not more remarkable than those which occurred between the courts of Common Law and Chancery at various periods in English history. On the other hand, the favour shown by the Spanish Crown to the Holy Office suggested to Soranzo, the Venetian ambassador in 1565, that an attempt was being made to use it to the detriment of other systems not enjoying the King's good-will; and the celebrated episode of Antonio Pérez, which occurred before the end of the century, gives colour to the suggestion.

Pérez, a protégé of the Prince of Eboli, the wisest of Philip II's counsellors, succeeded his patron as chief minister. Don John of Austria, who was endeavouring to reduce the revolted Netherlands to submission, in the summer of 1557 sent his secretary Escovedo to Madrid to ask for a more generous supply of the sinews of war. Pérez, who had long been endeavouring to poison the King's mind against Don John, persuaded him that the real object of Escovedo's mission was to foment a rebellion. Philip instructed his minister to arrange for Escovedo's murder, which took place on March 31, 1578. Pérez's guilt was suspected by many personages powerful at Court, and eventually the King found it expedient to disavow his minion and to sanction his prosecution. Under torture Pérez acknowledged his guilt but implicated the King. However, in April 1590 he succeeded in escaping from prison and as a native of Aragon he fled to Saragossa and there availed himself of the right of *manifestación*, i.e. that of appealing to be tried by the popular court of the *Justiza* instead of by one of the royal courts. This ancient privilege of his Aragonese subjects Philip could not override. It so happened that they were engaged in a violent dispute with him at this time, as they were resisting his determination to foist an alien Viceroy upon them, and in these circumstances Pérez was received with open arms. He was duly tried by the court of the *Justiza*, which pronounced his acquittal.

Philip was enraged and resolute not to be thwarted by the too independent Aragonese. When a number of trumped-up charges subsequently brought against Pérez had all alike failed, he decided to have recourse to the Inquisition. It was alleged that on his arrest the unfortunate man had used blasphemous words of despair and upon these was based an accusation of heresy. The Inquisitor-general ordered the arrest of Pérez, and, acting on his instructions, the tribunal in Saragossa demanded the surrender of his person, and as the right of *manifestación* did not extend to those indicted of heresy the *Justiza's* lieutenant handed over Pérez to the Inquisition. But the news of this produced so serious a rising of the mob in the city, who rose in defence of the *fueros* of the kingdom, that the magistrates, in order to keep the peace, persuaded the inquisitors to restore their prisoner into the custody of the *Justiza*.

But Aragon, by the action of the Saragossa populace, had put itself in the wrong, and the King seized with alacrity the opportunity presented to him. The inquisitors issued an edict setting forth the dire penalties to which all those who impeded the legitimate functions of the Holy Office exposed themselves. The nobles and all the cooler-headed members of the community dissociated themselves from the proceedings of the rabble, and it was decided that Pérez must once again be handed over to the Inquisition. But he still had powerful friends. There was a new ferment and he was rescued from his guards. Now rendered desperate, he began to intrigue for the formation of an independent Aragon republic under French protection. Finding no support for a scheme so revolutionary, he succeeded in escaping into French territory. The resistance of Saragossa completely collapsed. The young *Justiza*—his father had died during the progress of the Pérez case—was solemnly executed, and his court was brought under royal control. This triumph of the King was due solely to the adroit move of utilizing the one jurisdiction in the country against which the right of *manifestación* availed nothing.

CHAPTER IV

THE INQUISITORIAL PROCESS AND PENALTIES

BEFORE considering the most distinctive features of the inquisitional system of trial it will be well to enumerate briefly the main stages in the process.

Preliminary evidence was obtained by the devices of proclaiming a period of grace, which induced many to surrender themselves voluntarily in order to avail themselves of the milder treatment promised to those who did so, and of the Edict of Faith, which made it the solemn obligation of all good Christians, under the most dreadful anathemas, to give testimony concerning all cases of heresy and of other offences cognizable by the Holy Office of which they had knowledge. Evidence which was acquired either by such delation or by the general rumour or *diffamatio* of a neighbourhood or which was to be found in the writings of suspected persons was submitted to *calificadores*, who made a summary of it and gave an opinion as to whether it did or did not justify prosecution. In many cases, and indeed in the majority where Judaism, lapse into Mohammedanism, bigamy, etc., were alleged, this stage was omitted, the examination by censors being chiefly required where difficult questions of theology were involved.

If there seemed to be a *prima facie* case to warrant it, the fiscal then formally demanded the arrest of the accused.

Arrest by the Inquisition was apt to come like a bolt from the blue. It might take place in the middle of the night, the accused being awakened from sleep and led away to the secret prison of the Inquisition while in a state of confusion and bewilderment. In any case he knew neither the precise crime which had been alleged against him nor the identity of his accusers. His papers were seized, and if his alleged offence was of a serious nature, his property was immediately sequestrated, since in the event of his condemnation —which might not, however, occur for months or even years, if it occurred at all —it would be confiscated. The *alguazil* who made the arrest brought with him a notary, who made an inventory of the prisoner's possessions.

85

The secret prison to which the suspect was consigned was, as a rule, a much unpleasanter place than the *casa de penitencia* in which he would be immured were he to be condemned to a term of imprisonment, it being one of the curious anomalies of inquisitorial practice that the detention of the accused awaiting trial was generally more severe than that of the man condemned to imprisonment. The *cárceles secretas* were often dark, noisome, terrifying places infested with vermin, but others seem to have been comparatively clean, well lighted, ventilated and healthy. In some the inmates were given good and sufficient food and were properly tended by physicians when they were ill ; occasionally, on the other hand, there was gross neglect. In any case it is essential to bear in mind, when reading lurid accounts of the dungeons of the Spanish Inquisition, that their condition was no worse than that of most secular prisons not only in Spain but in other countries. Prison life anywhere was very dreadful according to modern standards prior to the reforms initiated by Beccaria and Howard.

It might be some considerable time after his consignment to the secret prison before the accused was definitely acquainted with the nature of the charge against him. Soon after his arrival he might be visited in his cell and asked if he was aware of the reason for his arrest, and he would be exhorted to confess any sins of which his conscience accused him. Certainly he would be adjured to do so at his first interview with the inquisitor, when he would be asked many questions concerning his place of domicile, his employment, his family, relatives, friends and teachers, and the places at which he had formerly resided. It was a rule that his answers must not be interrupted, and that they must all be carefully recorded. He would be asked to say the Lord's Prayer, the Pater Noster, the Ave Maria. This formality was useful for the detection of recent and merely nominal converts to Christianity, and was never omitted even in the case of learned and pious fathers of the Church. The accused might be confronted with the inquisitor at several audiences prior to his trial. The Inquisition could act with great celerity upon occasion, but more commonly its proceedings were very deliberate. Months might elapse between arrest and the·first audience and between one audience and another, and the whole process sometimes lasted for years.

It was only after these preliminary in-
terrogations that the fiscal formally presented his evidence and asked that the
latter should be ratified. The witnesses
were examined either by the inquisitor
himself or, more frequently, by a notary.
The ceremony of ratification took place
before two friars, known as *personas
honestas*, the prosecutor not being present,
and consisted in reading over their deposi-
tions to the witnesses, as a security against
inaccuracy or falsehood. If the probing
of the evidence was a reality, this practice
afforded some measure of protection to the
prisoner, but it seems often to have been
perfunctory.

The time had now arrived for the accused
to make his defence, and for this purpose
he was allowed counsel. This privilege
had not existed latterly in the medieval
Inquisition. The great inquisitors, Bernard Gui and Eymeric, had both laid it
down that defenders of those accused of
heresy rendered themselves liable to be
prosecuted as fautors of heretics, and few
can have been willing to take the risk
involved. In Spain, on the other hand,
the defendant was definitely assigned an
adviser. But the measure of protection
which this practice afforded was not very

great. The prisoner could not choose his own counsel, but had to select one from among two or three nominees of the court. Moreover, there was no conception that the adviser should act as a real advocate, and do his very utmost to discredit the evidence by closely cross-examining the witnesses and presenting his client's conduct in the most favourable light possible. He chiefly exerted himself to persuade his client to make his peace with the tribunal by making a full confession.

The conditions under which an inquisitorial trial was conducted precluded the possibility of a really thorough and strenuous defence. Any consultation between counsel and client had to take place before the inquisitor; as the names of the hostile witnesses were disclosed to neither of them and accusations were apt to be very deficient in precise details, they were both very much in the dark and had to proceed largely by guess-work. As had always been the case in the medieval Inquisition, the most hopeful line of defence was for the accused to name any enemies he had who might conceivably be filled with such malice as to prefer a false charge against him. If a mortal enemy of this description was found among the witnesses, his evidence was invalidated. But clearly this method of defence was drawing a bow at a venture—hit or miss. The defendant might also bring his own witnesses to testify to his good character, sound religious principle and practice. Again, he might plead extenuating circumstances —extreme youth, insanity, drunkenness or any similar incapacitating influence, or lack of heretical intent. But the Inquisition was always very suspicious of the plea of madness, and many poor wretches whom a modern judge would have no hesitation in sending to a lunatic asylum were sent by the inquisitor to the stake. In any case the plea of insanity was likely, and the denial of heretical intent was certain, to be tested by the use of torture.

After the accused had made the best answer to the charges within his power, there took place what was known as the *consulta de fe*—a consultation as to their verdict between the inquisitor, the bishop or his ordinary, and perhaps one or two theological or legal experts. Whenever they were at variance the Suprema was at hand to give a determining voice. As intervention by the Suprema in the affairs of the tribunals became more frequent, the importance of the *consulta de fe* greatly diminished, and latterly this stage in the inquisitorial trial was omitted. The *consulta* might either come to an immediate decision on the case or, if not satisfied with the evidence or in doubt for any other reason, it might have recourse to torture.

Torture was used when the accused had been inconsistent in his statements and this could not be accounted for either by stupidity or defective memory; when he had made only a partial confession; when he had acknowledged a wrongful act but denied heretical intent; when the evidence was itself defective. For example, it was a salutary maxim that two witnesses to the same act were necessary to prove heresy; but, on the other hand, the evidence of one witness, if supported by a general rumour or defamation, was sufficient to justify the application of torture. This reasoning had the curious consequence that the weaker the evidence for the prosecution, the more severe was the torture. It has, however, to be remembered that the alternative to torture was immediate condemnation.

The final stage of the trial was the formal pronouncement of sentence. For those found guilty of trivial offences this took place privately within the palace of the Inquisition ; but it was reserved for a great public ceremonial, or *auto de fe*, in the case of all serious crimes. The majority of those who were to appear at the *auto* were not apprised of the nature of their punishment until the morning of the event, when they were clothed in the distinctive garb which would enable the spectators to recognize the nature of their misdeeds ; but the most guilty of all, those who were to perish at the stake, received intimation the previous night in order to give them a last opportunity of confession and of saving their souls. Sentences might be pronounced either *con méritos* or *sin méritos*, i.e. either with or without a detailed catalogue of the crimes of which the prisoner had been found guilty. The latter were sometimes of inordinate length and occasionally took hours to read.

Such were the stages in a trial before the Spanish Inquisition. Its most notable features were the use of torture, the disadvantage under which the defence laboured, and the part played in the whole proceedings by the presiding inquisitor.

Much of the odium which was attached to the Spanish Inquisition in the popular mind has been due to its association with the cruelties of the torture-chamber. The idea of inflicting severe physical anguish in order to force confessions from a man on trial for his religious opinions revolts anyone of the slightest sensitiveness nowadays, and assuredly such repugnance can only be intensified by the perusal of the matter-of-fact relation in the inquisitorial records of all that occurred during the application of torture. Careful notes were taken, not only of all that was confessed by the victim, but of his shrieks, cries, lamentations, broken interjections and appeals for mercy. The most moving things in the literature of the Inquisition are not the accounts of their sufferings left by the victims but the sober memoranda kept by the officers of the tribunals. We are distressed and horrified just because there is no intention to shock us. The notary who methodically records these painful details has no conception that there is anything shocking about them. This attitude of detachment on his part is due, not to his being an officer of a persecuting tribunal, but to the fact that he lived in an age with different standards from ours.

In the Spanish Inquisition torture was occasionally applied to a witness if he shuffled in his evidence or retracted, while the prisoner could be tortured in the capacity of witness, *in caput alienum* to use the technical phrase, i.e. to elicit information regarding accomplices. No confession was considered complete unless it contained such intelligence. Thus a man who made voluntary admissions about himself might be put to the torture because he was unwilling to betray his friends.

The Spanish Inquisition is often credited with the invention of new refinements and eccentricities of cruelty; actually it appears to have been very conservative in its devices. It usually employed public executioners for the purpose, who used only the most familiar methods among the large variety practised in the secular courts. The commonest of all were those of the pulley and the *aselli*, or water-torture. The first consisted in tying the victim's hands behind his back, his wrists being fastened to a pulley or gibbet, by which he was hoisted from the floor. In severe applications weights of increasing size were attached to the feet, and the sufferer was held suspended for a while and then lowered with a jerk, which wrenched the whole body and every limb. The water-torture was probably worse.

The prisoner was placed on a sort of trestle, known as an *escalera* or ladder, with sharp-edged rungs across it, his head lying lower than his feet, in a hollowed-out trough and kept in position by an iron band round the forehead. Cords which cut into the flesh were twisted tightly round the arms, thighs and calves. The mouth was forcibly kept open and a strip of linen was forced into the throat, water being poured through this from a jar, so that throat and nostrils were stopped and a state of semi-suffocation was produced. These two forms of torture were displaced by others in the seventeenth century, supposed to be less injurious to life and limb, but hardly more endurable. For a considerable period before the abolition of the Inquisition the instruments of torment had become simply the disused relics of an evil past.

Before torture was applied, the victim was always examined by a physician, and severe disabilities usually procured postponement if not exemption.[1] On the other hand, neither youth nor age was a safeguard;

[1] The presiding inquisitor usually made a formal protest that if the victim died or suffered grievous bodily harm under the torture, this must be imputed, not to the Inquisition, but to the culprit himself for not telling the truth voluntarily.

old ladies of eighty and girls in their teens were alike placed on the rack. The whole business of the torture-chamber was carried out with the utmost deliberation. As soon as the victim had been brought into the room and the horrific masked figure of the executioner had made his appearance, he was earnestly adjured to save himself by making a free confession. If he refused, he was stripped naked save for a short pair of trunk drawers, and again urged to confess. He was then bound, and the adjuration was once more repeated. Only if the prisoner still remained obdurate did the torture itself commence. It proceeded slowly so that the maximum effect was obtained from each twist and jar. It was a rule that no specific questions were to be addressed to the culprit while on rack or pulley, but everything that he uttered —however inarticulate—was noted down. It was also a rule that torture must never be repeated, but as had happened in the medieval tribunals, so in those of Spain, this prohibition was casuistically overcome by the transparent subterfuge of describing a second or third application as a continuation of the first. Confessions made under torture had to be ratified within twenty-four hours outside the chamber of torment and without the use of threats. It must not be supposed that torture was an invariable concomitant of inquisitorial trials; probably in the majority of cases it was not found necessary, and it was not allowed in the trial of a large number of minor offences which came within the Inquisition's purview.

Some of the disabilities under which the defendant laboured have already been mentioned. The protection afforded by the ratification of evidence for the prosecution and by the provision of counsel was largely illusory. Never since its inception in the thirteenth century had the Inquisition in any country been fair to the prisoner in the matter of evidence. Evidence from a kinsman was accepted if it was hostile; but never if it was favourable. Criminals, excommunicates, all sorts of undesirable persons were freely heard against the prisoner, but Jews, Moors, servants of the prisoner, though of the most respectable character, could not give testimony for him. The refusal to disclose the identity of his accusers was, however, his most serious disability. Inquisitor-general Manrique was at first in favour of publishing the names, but, being assured that this step would lead to a great increase in the number of Judaizers and be prejudicial to the success of the Inquisition, he withdrew the suggestion.

Finally, defence was difficult because the Inquisition was not an ordinary court of justice and the inquisitor was not an ordinary judge. The Holy Office claimed to be the most merciful of all tribunals because its aim was not the administration of a stern and automatic justice but the reconciliation of the offender. With the Holy Office to plead guilty was to obtain mercy ; of what other court could that be said ? The inquisitor was as much a father-confessor as a judge, aiming not at condemnation but at ending an estrangement, at restoring erring lambs to the fold. The accused was, therefore, constantly urged to remember the fundamental difference between the Inquisition and ordinary courts of law, in that its object was not the punishment of the body but the saving of the soul, and he was therefore adjured to seek salvation through confession.

This attitude presupposed that there was some degree of guilt to be confessed ; and one may fairly put it that the inquisitorial point of view was that there could be no smoke without fire. Even those whose innocence was made clear during the course of an inquisitorial trial were almost always reprimanded for having been so remiss or imprudent as to get themselves into trouble ; the conduct of a good Catholic should be such as never to expose him to suspicion. The Spanish, like the medieval Inquisition, treated the incurring of suspicion as an offence, and it was punished in proportion to its seriousness, as *light, moderate,* or *strong.* Thus it was exceedingly difficult for a man who had been brought before the Holy Office to leave it literally without a stain upon his character. If there was the very remotest doubt of his complete innocence, he was declared to be lightly suspect. It used to be said : " A man may leave the Inquisition without being burnt, but he is sure to be singed."

The Holy Office, not being a mere court of law which inexorably awarded requital for wrong-doing, but a means for the saving of souls, did not, strictly speaking, punish, but simply imposed penances appropriate to the gravity of the sin which had been admitted as outward and visible signs of repentance. Thus, the penitent who had incurred suspicion was required to swear with his face turned to the cross and with his hand on the gospels that he held the Catholic faith and detested heretics, and that he would cheerfully undergo any penance enjoined upon him; and, if the suspicion had been strong, he had furthermore to add that he desired if he failed to perform his penance that he should be treated as one who had relapsed. Now, the penalty for relapse was burning, and no new trial was necessary. Abjuration *de vehementi*, as it was called, was, therefore, a very solemn and terrible thing.

The Inquisition occasionally enjoined purely spiritual penances for the more venial offences, such as frequent and regular fasting and the making of pilgrimages to S. Iago de Compostela and other shrines; but the latter kind of penance, common in the practice of the medieval Inquisition, was rare in Spain. Exile for periods varying from a month or two to a lifetime was much more frequently imposed—it might be simply from the culprit's own town or village, or from a whole district, or even from the country altogether. This was a serious punishment, which obviously might involve the ruination of a man's professional or business career.

Flogging was still more often ordered.

100

Penitents sentenced to this penalty were mounted astride on donkeys, bare to the waist, round their necks a halter, on their heads a mitre on which was inscribed a record of their offence. They were led solemnly through the streets, while the executioner plied a leather strap upon their backs, a notary keeping a tally of the strokes and a town-crier proclaiming that the punishment was by order of the Holy Office. The great majority of sentences to the scourge were for 200 lashes. Neither age nor sex was spared. In Valencia in 1607 an old man of eighty-six and a girl of thirteen each received 100 lashes. In the eighteenth century there was a reaction against this penalty, and while sometimes ordained, it was in practice commonly remitted. Sometimes the culprit was merely paraded bare-backed, with halter and mitre, and not scourged. This lesser penance was known as *vergüenza*, or humiliation.

Imprisonment was the commonest of major penalties, the period of incarceration varying from a few months to a lifetime. But a sentence of life imprisonment *cum misericordia* could be remitted and the offender might look for release in five years or less. Even a nominally irremissible life

101

sentence seldom involved confinement for
more than eight years. It appears that
the resources of the Inquisition were
severely taxed to find the necessary accommodation, while it was reluctant to spend
money on the building and maintenance of
a large number of gaols. In its early days,
when persecution was on a large scale,
there are actually cases of prisoners being
allowed to serve their time in private
houses, occasionally even in their own.
Detention in such cases can have been no
great hardship and often little more than
nominal.

It was because of the lack of sufficient
prison accommodation, and also perhaps
to satisfy the king's demands for forced
labour, that the Inquisition sometimes
sentenced culprits to the galleys. A bull
of Alexander VI of 1503 sanctioned this
penalty for heresy on the ground that if
heretics were placed in ordinary gaols they
might pervert other inmates. The humanitarianism of the eighteenth century led
to the ruling that no one was to be sent
to the galleys unless he had been pronounced physically fit by a doctor.
Labour at the oar was a very heavy
punishment, much worse than duress in a
penitentiary prison.

Everyone who appeared as a penitent at an *auto de fe* had to wear a habit, generally known as a *sanbenito*, appropriate to his crime. This system goes back to the very early days of the medieval Inquisition, the Councils of Narbonne (1229) and Béziers (1233) having laid down elaborate regulations as to these garments. In Torquemada's time they were all of them black, but latterly that colour was reserved for obdurate and relapsed heretics (there being lurid delineations upon them of fiery flames or of demons thrusting the wicked into hell), while the other *sanbenitos* were yellow, with red or saffron St. Andrew's crosses worked on back and chest. In addition to clothing all their culprits in this garb of ignominy on the great occasion of the *auto de fe*, the tribunals frequently enjoined the constant wearing of a *sanbenito* for a given period as a penance. This was no light punishment, for it exposed the wearer to derision or insult, when he was abroad in the street or at his work. The Inquisition also required that after the time of penance had been fulfilled the *sanbenito* should not be destroyed but hung up in the parish church, as a lasting memorial of the shame which the wearer had incurred, and as a warning to his descendants. Nay, more, when the habits themselves perished from age, they had to be replaced by strips of yellow linen bearing the names, family, crime and punishment of the offender. The Inquisition plainly attached great value to the *sanbenito* system, and one of the duties of an inquisitor when he made his periodical circuits of his districts was to see that the *sanbenitos* and the linen strips were duly retained in the churches. Not unnaturally attempts were often made to hide or to steal these lasting emblems of shame.

Punishment by the Inquisition involved automatically a number of serious disabilities for the culprit and his family, notably exclusion from office under the State, and the confiscation of property by the State. A wife's dowry was not regarded as forfeited on account of her husband's heresy, and the Spanish Inquisition, unlike that of the Middle Ages, usually recognized that properly proved debts were a first charge upon the confiscated estates. Torquemada ruled that a small portion of the culprit's goods might be utilized by the inquisitors for the support and education of his children. Peña, one of the chief authorities on inquisitorial procedure, held that the sons of heretics ought to be apprenticed to mechanical trades, and their daughters put into service in the households of ladies of unexceptionable religious reputation. On the other hand, Simancas, a still greater authority, contemplated the beggary of the children of heretics with equanimity, and even regarded it as being for the public welfare. Another inquisitor justified the punishment of children as well as parents because heresy was a crime not merely against man but against God. Even allowing for such alleviations as were granted, the system of confiscation inflicted a great deal of suffering upon many innocent persons, and it is hardly possible to exaggerate the damage done to the economic welfare of the country. Among those whose property was thus seized upon in the days of Ferdinand and Charles V were rich Marranos and Moriscos, whose wealth was being productively used in trade and industry. Among their possessions were merchandise and ships as well as houses, furniture and personal belongings. When such things were liable to instant seizure, not only was the course of business disorganized, but credit was severely shaken.

Torquemada gave instructions that those

who voluntarily surrendered within the time of grace should be exempt from confiscation, but liable to amercement. As time went on and the victims of the Inquisition came to be drawn from less wealthy classes, the imposition of fines became commoner as the normal penalty for such offences as impeding the work of the Holy Office, bigamy, blasphemy, assisting heretics, and for suspicion of heresy.

The zeal of persecution has often been attributed to cupidity. There is more point in this accusation when it is brought against the Spanish than against the medieval Inquisition, since a considerable proportion of the heretics of Spain were wealthy people, whereas the vast majority of medieval sectaries were poor, certainly not worth harrying for the sake of their worldly goods. Nevertheless, religious persecution cannot be ascribed simply to mercenary motives in either case. On the other hand, the large part which financial penalties play in inquisitorial proceedings show the importance attached to them. Not only was the machinery of persecution maintained out of the proceeds, but very large sums went into the royal exchequer.

106

The final and most terrible punishment for heresy was that of the stake. Just as the Inquisition never sentenced an offender to the forfeiture of his property, so it never condemned anyone to death. What the Inquisition did was to relax the impenitent to the secular arm. It was by the authority of the State and in accordance with its laws that the heretic was executed. The inquisitors do their utmost to save the offender by incessant argument and exhortation; only when this fervent effort to save has been met by utter obduracy do they withdraw their sheltering arms and allow him to fall into the hands of the temporal power, which will deal with him not in accordance with the long-suffering patience of the Church but with strict and impartial justice. Such is the theory underlying the sentence of " relaxation to the secular arm." Mother Church cannot spill the blood of even the most recalcitrant of her children. But while it is essential to grasp the fact that heretics were burnt by the State, not by the Inquisition, it is equally essential not to be misled by this into imagining that the Inquisition thereby escapes all moral responsibility in the matter. Only the ignorant apologist for the Holy Office

107

H

makes so gross and so stupid an error as to suggest this. The sentence of relaxation was equivalent to a sentence of death and the inquisitor in pronouncing it knew this. There was no possible escape. The secular authorities would accept the verdict and undertake the punishment for which " relaxation " was the universally understood euphemism, and an officer of the Inquisition would be present at the burning to report to his tribunal that it had taken place. To visit the obdurate heretic with any penalty less than death would have been to stultify the whole inquisitorial system. To scourge and imprison the penitent and then fail to secure that the impenitent met a worse fate would have been as fatuous as unjust. So, when the inquisitor in relaxing the heretic to the secular arm prayed that he might be treated with benignity, everyone concerned knew that this was an empty formula and that those who used it would have been righteously indignant had it been taken seriously.

For the inquisitor was sincerely convinced that there could be no greater scandal than to suffer the impenitent heretic to live. He interpreted literally the words in the Fourth Gospel : " If a man abide not in me, he is cast forth as a branch, and is withered; and men gather them, and cast them into the fire, and they are burned." [1] Carena argues that since burning is the most terrible of all deaths it is fitting that the most grievous of crimes should be punished with it; if a more terrible punishment could be devised, it would have to be employed. Such was the point of view of the zealous inquisitor in Spain in the sixteenth century; it was shared by the zealous magistrate and the zealous citizen.

Relaxation was reserved for five classes of culprit. First, there was the pertinacious heretic, who acknowledged his false doctrines and refused up to the last to recant. There were not many such, especially after the first frenzy of persecution had died out early in the sixteenth century and inquisitors made persistent efforts to secure confession. Secondly, there was the *negativo*, the man who persistently denied that he held any erroneous beliefs when the tribunal was satisfied that he did. Peña solemnly propounds the problem

[1] The Sicilian inquisitor, Ludovico à Paramo, was not very happily inspired in finding warrant for the stake in James and John calling down fire upon the Samaritans, the heretics of their day!

whether it is permissible for a good Catholic, faced by the danger of the stake, to make what he conceives to be a false confession. He decides that it is not. The *negativo* was a man, who, holding himself to be a good Catholic and no heretic (whether rightly or wrongly), came to the same conclusion. Llorente declared that nine-tenths of those condemned by the Spanish Inquisition were good Catholics, but that is a fantastic exaggeration. There was also the *diminuto,* one whose confession was deemed to be inadequate— who, for example, admitted having committed certain acts but would not acknowledge that they betokened heresy. Much the most numerous class of those delivered over to the secular arm were the relapsed —namely, those who having recanted and having been reconciled fell back into their former errors. With these there must also be included culprits who, having abjured *de vehementi* failed to carry out the penances enjoined upon them, and who were therefore, to use the words of Simancas, rightly punished as " impenitent, perjured and feigned converts."

There were, finally, persons who were relaxed by the Spanish Inquisition, but who would have escaped in the Middle

Ages. In those days no one who was prepared to make complete abjuration paid the ultimate penalty. Simancas was of opinion that the heresiarch, the man who not merely holds erroneous beliefs himself but instils them into other people, was guilty of an unpardonable offence and ought not to be reconciled, however repentant he might be. Paul IV held the same view and gave the Inquisitor-general instructions to this effect in 1559. Apart altogether from the special case of heresiarchs, the Spanish Inquisition was more chary about accepting last-minute repentances than the medieval Inquisition. Eymeric relates the episode of a heretic who, being actually amidst the flames, cried out that he would abjure, and was immediately released from the fire. Such an incident could not have happened from the days of Ferdinand and Isabella onwards. The *Instrucciónes Antiguas* laid it down that if relaxation was to be avoided confession must be made before the final sentence, and the *Instrucciónes Nuevas* draw attention to the undesirability of reconciling those who delayed their recantation till the *auto de fe*, as it was probably inspired by fear rather than by contrition. Nevertheless, at this ceremony a room was always

111

provided under the platform to which one whose obduracy gave way at any moment prior to the actual reading of his sentence could be transferred, relaxation being commuted to perpetual imprisonment and additional penalties; while even for the prisoner who delayed his confession till after formal sentence there was a measure of mercy. Instead of being burnt alive he was strangled before his body was tied to the stake.

Certainly less reluctance to burn the heretic was shown in Spain than in other countries in which the Inquisition flourished. The number of those who suffered it is utterly impossible to tell owing to the fragmentary character of the accurate information available. Llorente put the total at nearly 32,000, but his method of calculation is fantastic and ridiculous. All that can be done is to consider the figures which exist for particular tribunals and for limited periods. Out of over 2,000 sentences pronounced by the Toledo tribunal between 1575 and 1610 only 15 were of relaxation in person, while there were 185 of confiscation, 175 of imprisonment, 167 of exile, and 133 of scourging. Out of 3,000 sentences pronounced at various *autos* between 1721 and

1727 there were 77 to relaxation in person.[1]
Burnings were certainly a great deal more
numerous in the early years of the Inquisition, but no statistics were kept then.
It may, however, be noted that del Pulgar,
a secretary to Queen Isabella, whose
chronicle comes down to 1490, gave the
number of heretics burnt as 2,000 ; and
that Zurita estimates that prior to 1520 as
many as 4,000 had perished in Seville
alone.

The great public event which showed
forth the might of the Inquisition was
the *auto de fe*. Celebrated with greater
pomp in Spain than in Rome itself, the
ceremony attracted enormous crowds,
brought thither by religious enthusiasm,
curiosity or the desire to earn the forty
days' indulgence with which it was customary to reward attendance. A feast-day
was commonly selected for the ceremony
and proclamation made a month before-
hand. Familiar is Voltaire's gibe that an
Asiatic, arriving in Madrid on such an
occasion, would be doubtful whether he was
witnessing a festival, a religious ceremony,

[1] See *Catalogo de las Causas contra la fe seguidas
ante el Tribunal del Santo Officio de Toledo* (Madrid,
1903), pp. 6–330. Summarized in Lea, Vol. III,
pp. 551–4.

a sacrifice or a massacre : it was in fact
all of these. On the evening prior to the
auto a procession wended its way through
the streets of the town to the square in
which the necessary staging had already
been erected, and above the altar on the
platform was deposited the Green Cross,
which was the emblem of the Inquisition.
Another cross was carried to the burning-
place, known as the *quemadero* or *brasero*.

Very early next morning the culprits
were assembled in the prison of the Inquisition, arrayed in their *sanbenitos*, and
given food to sustain them during the
prolonged ceremony. The procession was
then formed. First came halberdiers ; then
the cross of the parish church shrouded in
black. Next followed the penitents, accompanied by halberdiers and familiars,
those to be lightly penanced leading,
those to be relaxed in rear. There were
also borne aloft effigies of heretics whom
it had not been possible to bring in person
—either because they had succeeded in
making good their escape or because they
had died before their errors were discovered. These effigies would be burnt,
so that, if the grave or flight abroad saved
the culprits from the pains of death, it
should not relieve their children of the

114

shame of having fathers who had been relaxed and from suffering the consequent disabilities. After the effigies came a number of secular officials and distinguished familiars, then the banner of the Inquisition with its green cross on a sable field, adorned with a branch of green olive on the right side symbolizing mercy, and on the left the drawn sword of justice. Finally, behind this standard came the inquisitors themselves.

The proceedings opened with a sermon, after which was read aloud the oath of allegiance to the Holy Office, which was supposed to be taken by all present. There followed the reading of the sentences alternately from two pulpits on either side of the staging—usually a very lengthy proceeding. Each penitent, as his name was called, was led forward and remained standing while his sentence was read. Then upon his knees he received absolution, and the chief inquisitor pronounced him to be released from excommunication. At the conclusion of the proceedings he was taken back to the prison of the Inquisition. On the morrow he would be transferred to the penitentiary prison or handed over to the custody of the State prior to his being sent to the galleys or, maybe, flogged through the streets. While the reconciled were returning to their cells, the recalcitrant, mounted upon donkeys, under the guardianship of the royal officer and accompanied by confessors, were led out to the place of burning.

Public *autos*, being expensive, were of infrequent occurrence, especially in the period of the Inquisition's decay, and years might elapse between one such celebration and another in any particular city. The ordinary private *autos* were usually held inside a church, attended by as many of the general public as could find room, but not by secular functionaries in their official capacity. In the great days of the Inquisition it was regarded as essential that there should be a public *auto* whenever there were prisoners to be relaxed, it being regarded as unseemly that relaxation should take place inside sacred precincts ; but in the eighteenth century this difficulty was overcome by the representative of the secular arm being present in the church simply to hear the sentences read and then proceeding to an agreed rendezvous where the victims were handed over to him to be conveyed to the *brasero*. Gone were those stupendous spectacles, arranged sometimes as celebrations of royal mar-

116

riages or the state visits of kings, which were outward and visible demonstrations of the religious faith and doctrinal unity of the Spanish people.

CHAPTER V

MORISCOS AND MARRANOS

THE Spanish Inquisition, as it was re-created by Ferdinand and Isabella, was the outcome of three factors—the determination to achieve religious uniformity in Spain despite its large Jewish and Moorish population, the failure of the policy of enforced conversion to effect this purpose, and the fear that half-measures might simply lead to the contamination of Christianity, that insincere Christians would pervert true Christians.

So far as the Moriscos are concerned the story of the use of the Holy Office for this purpose can be told quite briefly, since the experience of a little over a century was sufficient to persuade the Spanish Government in 1609 that it could not assimilate this alien population, and that it must be ejected. Whether the converted Moors of Granada became Christians in anything more than name or had an opportunity of learning anything at all about their new religion depended very largely upon whether they came in contact with missionaries suffused with the spirit of Talavera or merely with ecclesiastical authorities content to enforce attendance at Mass. At the time of the conquest the inhabitants of Granada had been promised freedom from the presence of the Inquisition for a period of forty years. That much time was vouchsafed to them in which to become so conversant with the creed of Christianity that thereafter error could be deemed a crime. But this promise was not fulfilled. When Charles V visited Granada in 1526 complaints were made to him of the ill-treatment of priests as well as of officials, and a gloomy picture was drawn of the state of Christianity among the Moriscos. The upshot was the issue of an edict by Manrique, the Inquisitor-general, establishing a tribunal in Granada. While an amnesty was granted for past offences and a term of grace was allowed during which voluntary confessions would be accepted, it was intimated that thereafter the laws against heresy would be rigorously enforced.

So far as the Moorish inhabitants of other parts of Spain were concerned, ever since 1510 Edicts of Grace had from time to time been issued in consideration of the fact that many had fallen into error through lack of adequate instruction, and confessions within the stipulated period had been received without entailing the usual consequences of confiscation and public abjuration. But those who did not avail themselves of this privilege were liable to delation by private informers, and for all alike, whether they incriminated themselves or were incriminated by others, relapse involved the same awful penalties. Thus, while the Moors in Granada had been free from molestation, persecution had been rife among their compatriots scattered abroad in other parts of Spain. Inquisitors had been quick to discern the evidence of backsliding into Mohammedanism in such indications as abstinence from wine or from pork, and the use of characteristic Moorish songs and dances at marriages and other festivals. For the instruction of the faithful lists of Moorish customs and of other signs denoting the Muslim were included in edicts of faith, so as to facilitate the recognition and denunciation of symptoms of backsliding. As a result of the work of the Inquisition the Moriscos were reduced to outward conformity in many parts of Spain, especially in Castile, where many of them abandoned their native dress and language.

In 1526 a similar abandonment of native customs was enforced upon Granada, but this occasioned such consternation that it was suspended. At first the Inquisition established in Granada was not very formidable ; it did not hold its first *auto* till 1529 and then only three Moriscos were sentenced. It was not until the reign of Philip II that the Moriscos of Granada found themselves in serious straits. The change of policy on the part of the Government which then took place was undoubtedly due to the serious attacks then being made by Barbary pirates on shipping in the Mediterranean and on Spanish coast-towns, and to the not unnatural fears of correspondence between the Moriscos and their dangerous brethren in northern Africa. From time to time wild rumours were current that the Berbers would invade the country in great numbers and, with the help of the Moriscos, re-establish Mohammedan rule in Spain. There were certainly plots among the Moriscos, and Henry IV of France toyed with the idea of entering into an alliance with them for the embarrassment of his Habsburg foe.

Philip II decided to revive the policy of the 1526 edict. There were to be no more of the baths, the songs and the dances in which the Moors delighted; no weddings were to be celebrated save with Christian ritual; women must not go about the streets with their faces covered; after the lapse of three years the use of Arabic was not to be allowed. Behind this policy stood Espinosa, the new Inquisitor-general, and the enforcement of it was entrusted to a member of the Suprema named Deza. The result of his efforts was a great Morisco rebellion, which broke out in December 1568. Though hopeless from the first, nevertheless it was not finally crushed till after prolonged military operations conducted by Don John of Austria—in 1571. Long before the pacification was complete Deza suggested that the Moorish inhabitants of Granada should be removed to other parts of Spain, where instead of forming a single community they could be scattered abroad among the Old Christians. Despite the inherent difficulties of the operation it was carried out with such thoroughness that at an *auto de fe* in Granada in 1593 only one out of 81 culprits was charged with secret Mohammedanism.

Special mention should be made of the Moors in Valencia, who were implicated in the *Germania* of 1520–2. During that civil war and immediately after it many were forced to receive baptism. There was also a considerable amount of zealous missionary enterprise. In September 1525 Charles V published his will that no Muslim should remain within the kingdom of Aragon. More wholesale baptisms followed, and, while the great majority of the Valencian Moors remained in the country, it was soon possible to say that the kingdom of Aragon was at last wholly Christian. It was realized that the new converts could not be expected forthwith to abandon customs which had become habits, and they, like their compatriots in Granada, were promised immunity from the Inquisition for a space of forty years. But again, as in the case of Granada, the undertaking was violated. Secular authority might be prepared to wait for the gradual eradication of national usages, but the Inquisition was not, if this meant condoning heathen practices. There were numerous prosecutions for Islamism before ten years had elapsed, and, if the Moors enjoyed exemption from confiscation of their property, they were often so heavily

123

fined that total forfeiture would not have been a great deal worse. Persecution was very extensive in the last few years of the sixteenth century. At last, in August 1599, Philip III issued an edict giving errant Moriscos of Valencia a final chance of voluntary confession. The complete failure of the edict sealed the fate of the Moriscos of Spain. The King and his advisers in April, 1609, decided in favour of their expulsion. Granted that this wholesale banishment was to take place at all, the conditions were comparatively merciful—the exiles being allowed to take away with them such of their worldly goods as they could carry, and ships being provided for their transport to Africa. The expulsion was not universal, those who had for two years comported themselves as good Christians and who had been admitted to Communion, and also the Moorish wives of Old Christians and their children, being permitted to remain. By 1615 the process of deporting the Morisco inhabitants from all parts of Spain had been virtually completed. Their going deprived the country of many of its most skilful, most industrious and best-disciplined workers—it was a great economic disaster—nevertheless, the Spaniards heaved a sigh of relief at their departing. Once more the incompatibility of Spanish Christianity with any sort of deviation from it had been signally demonstrated.

While the eviction of the Moriscos automatically solved the problem of the half-hearted convert from Islam to Christianity when the Inquisition had been in existence for about 130 years, the problem of the heretical Jewish Converso remained almost as long as the Inquisition did. At the opening of the sixteenth century the Suprema was following the policy of scattering among the Old Christians those Marranos who had been converted prior to 1492, the year of the expulsion of the Jews, and congregating those who had been converted since that date in towns where they could be under supervision, separated from their own rabbis, and compelled to be punctual in their religious observances. Just as inquisitors were keenly on the alert to descry the most trivial evidence of relapse into Mohammedanism, so also they were on the look out for similar tokens of relapse into Judaism—such as putting on fresh linen and clean clothes on a Saturday, giving a child a Hebrew name, eating meat during Lent, fasting on the Jewish Day of Atonement, eating unleavened bread. The hostility towards the Hebrews felt by the Old Christians still provided a sufficient number of informers to enable the Inquisition to bring offenders to justice. In 1531 Erasmus speaks of Spain as being as full of Jews as Germany is of robbers; but they were even then being rapidly driven by systematic persecution into an abandonment of even the most secret practice of their ancient faith. There is a very big decrease in the number of cases of Judaism brought before the tribunals in the second half of the sixteenth century. It seemed indeed as though Judaism had been stamped out of Spain altogether.

But in the year 1580 Philip II conquered Portugal, and as a result a new phase opened in the history of the Spanish Inquisition and the Jews. As the result of the dynastic connection now established between the two Iberian countries, a large number of keen traders of Jewish race left Portugal and settled in the wealthier kingdom. Many of these were secret Judaizers. When the Jews had been expelled from Spain in 1492, 90,000 of them had found refuge across the Tagus, John II admitting them for what was at first

126

intended to be only a temporary sojourn at the price of a high capitation tax. Under his successor many Jews found conversion expedient, while there were numerous cases of the forcible baptism of Jewish children. The opening years of the sixteenth century were very miserable in Portugal. Bad harvests led to famine, and famine was followed by plague. Hatred and credulity found in the Jews an explanation of these disasters, and in 1506 the mob of Lisbon perpetrated a terrible massacre among them, some 2,000 perishing. After this outrage there was a revulsion of feeling, but the next sovereign, John III, was a fanatical foe of the Hebrew race, and it was his ambition to secure for his country an Inquisition on the Spanish model. After considerable delays he obtained the necessary papal brief in 1536, but many restrictions were at first imposed on the liberty of action of the new institution, and it was not till 1547 that these trammels were removed. When Portugal was conquered in 1580 the two Inquisitions were not amalgamated, but the Portuguese tribunals, which had been quite active already, were stirred to still greater energy. The thoroughness of the persecution of Judaizers which was being carried on in the smaller kingdom was an added inducement for Jewish traders to migrate into Spain. It was true that there was an Inquisition there also, but of late it had not been greatly troubling the Jews, and, besides, the new-comers were less well known than in the country they had left.

In 1604 the Portuguese New Christians succeeded in making a bargain with Philip III. In return for the payment of a very large sum they obtained special terms, which were sanctioned by a papal brief in August. Those resident in Europe who came forward within the next twelve months, those outside Europe who did so within two years, were to be reconciled with the imposition of spiritual penances only. But the immunity so purchased was not lasting, and there was a recrudescence of persecution in Portugal at the opening of the reign of Philip IV. This was followed by an extensive new influx of Jews into Castile. The rigour of the Portuguese tribunals at this time seems to have been such that emigration into Spain afforded the prospect of greater security. But anti-Semitism was very intense in Spain also in the seventeenth century. A treatise written by an inquis-

itor in 1632 ascribes the decay of Portugal
—which had in fact been largely due to
the Spanish conquest—to the corrupting
influence of the Jews, who are now in
similar fashion undermining the Spanish
character and having a deleterious character upon the country's industry, especially its agriculture. There were fanatics
who believed that the Jewish race was
irreclaimable and that, hostility to Christianity being in their blood, converted Jews
could only be insincere and an insidious
danger to the faith of true Christians.
The persecution of the Conversos continued with ferocity during the seventeenth century, nearly all the victims
being Portuguese who had migrated into
Spain at various dates since 1580.

One of the worst outbreaks was, however, directed against native Spanish Jews.
This was the great Majorcan persecution
of the years 1678 to 1691. For about
150 years the tribunal in that island had
been singularly inert, and in consequence
the Jewish population had lived for the
most part unmolested; but in 1678 an
inquisitor discovered a congregation of
Jews in a garden outside Palma. He came
to the conclusion that this was a meeting for the worship of the synagogue,

and the Inquisition sprang to life again. The prosecutions that followed were remarkable for the fact that there were no burnings—since confessions were spontaneous—but large confiscations of property. In 1691, however, 37 who had relapsed since their reconciliation in 1679 were executed—three were burnt alive, the remainder were strangled before their bodies were committed to the flames.

After this the Majorcan tribunal relapsed into tranquillity. But in Castile, where the great majority of the Portuguese Jews had settled, and also in Andalusia, there continued to be many prosecutions for Judaism ; the large majority of the cases brought before the tribunals there being for that offence. The preponderance is very marked in the second decade of the eighteenth century, when Judaism was practically monopolizing the attention of the Inquisition. While the Jews inside the country were being harried, the Government were endeavouring to prevent any more from coming in. It is noteworthy that Clause X of the Treaty of Utrecht, wherein Spain handed over Gibraltar to Great Britain, contained a stipulation " that no leave shall be given, under any pretence whatsoever, either to Jews or Moors, to reside, or have their dwellings in the said town of Gibraltar." The combined effect of the zealous persecution of Conversos, who betrayed any sign of continued allegiance to the religion of Jehovah, and the exclusion of people of Jewish race was from the point of view of the Inquisition very satisfactory. Judaism was driven underground, and it was only by taking the most elaborate precautions that it was able to continue to exist at all even upon the smaller scale and in the most attenuated form. But it was never entirely uprooted, and at the opening of the nineteenth century the Inquisition was still dealing with a few isolated cases.

CHAPTER VI

PROTESTANTS

THE persecution of Protestants bulks large in popular accounts of the Spanish Inquisition, some of which contain little else but a narrative of the trials of Lutherans and a few picturesque tales about Escovedo and Pérez and, quite irrelevantly, of Philip II's unhappy insane son Don Carlos. Preoccupation with the episode of Spanish Lutheranism is to be found both in works of a strongly Protestant bias and in others written by Catholic apologists for the Holy Office. The former concentrate upon it to the virtual exclusion of the story of Moriscos and Jews because they are not interested in them; the latter do so because it is perhaps easier to defend the Inquisition's treatment of the Lutherans than that of its most numerous victims. Such concentration is misleading, for the episode of Spanish Protestantism forms a brief and relatively unimportant chapter in the history of the institution. The Jews suffered from Spanish intolerance during the whole three centuries and more of that history, and many thousands of them fell victims to it; the Lutheran movement in Spain, on the other hand, was virtually stamped out in thirty or forty years with the sacrifice of a few hundred lives. But while it is essential to remember how small a proportion of the prisoners who appeared before the Inquisition were Protestants, the story of the Spanish Lutherans has very great inherent interest.

The first measure taken to prevent the spread of Lutheran doctrines in the Peninsula was the order issued in April 1521 by Adrian of Utrecht, then Inquisitor-general, ordering the seizure of Lutheran books. But as yet there was no hint of obscurantism. Erasmus at first had many admirers in Spain, such as Manrique, Adrian's successor as Inquisitor-general, and Fonseca, the Archbishop of Toledo. Ten years later, however, the devotees of Erasmus found themselves in peril. If he appealed strongly to men of learning, he antagonized the very much more numerous monks and friars of limited intelligence whom he satirized in his *Praise of Folly*. His ridicule and his criticisms might with reason be resented in Spain,

133

where the standard of zeal and purity of life among both regular and secular clergy was much higher than in Germany or in Italy, largely as the result of the notable reforms carried out by two Inquisitors-general, Ximenes and Adrian. The Spanish opponents of Erasmus also felt that the brilliant Fleming was unsound in doctrine, and they demanded the condemnation of certain of his views. With the death of Fonseca the latter party tended to get the upper hand. Juan de Vergara, a friend of both Ximenes and Fonseca, Professor of Philosophy in the University of Alcalá, who was one of the most prominent of the followers of Erasmus in Spain, was brought before the Inquisition on the charge of being a defender of heretics. It was alleged that he possessed Lutheran books and held certain Lutheran tenets. After a most protracted trial he had to abjure *de vehementi*. Another *Erasmista*, a Benedictine abbot named Virués, despite the intervention of Charles V, with whom he was a favourite preacher, languished for four years in prison before the Inquisition finally decided that he also was suspect of Lutheranism. Neither Vergara nor Virués, it is interesting to note, was prejudiced in his subsequent carecr by

134

the humiliation of having to make public abjuration, and the latter actually became a bishop. They were, indeed, simply learned men, whose scholarship made them sympathetic to Erasmus, and certainly not adherents of Luther.

A number of the most illustrious Spaniards who were really Lutherans lived outside the Peninsula and so did not figure at any *auto de fe*, except possibly in effigy. Such was Francisco de Enzinas, better known as Dryander, who left Spain before he embraced reformed opinions. Still more notable was Juan de Valdés, a friend of Pietro Vermigli and Bernardino Ochino, the principal Italian reformers, who spent the latter years of his life in Naples. There may also be mentioned Juan Pérez de Pineda, who was a pastor at Geneva and at Blois; Juan Díaz, who assisted Bucer at the second Colloquy of Ratisbon in 1546; and Antonio del Corro, who was at one time preacher to the Spanish Protestants in London and taught theology at Oxford.

Protestantism inside Spain centred in two communities, in Seville and Valladolid. Except in those cities and their neighbourhoods it was negligible, although the first important Spanish reformer who was brought to the stake was, like Enzinas, a native of Burgos. This was Francisco de San Roman, who imbibed Protestant opinions as the result of a casual visit to a Lutheran church in Antwerp. He became an intemperate fanatic and threw all caution to the winds. He was imprisoned as a heretic in Ratisbon by Charles V's orders and then sent to Spain, where he perished, the crowd at the *brasero* demonstrating their detestation of the Lutheran schismatic by piercing him with their swords.

The founder of the community at Seville was the learned Juan Gil, known as Egidio, who had been converted to reformed opinions by a certain Rodrigo de Valer, a man of wealth and good family, who is said to have preached heresies and inveighed against evils in the Church in the public streets, but to have been leniently treated by the Inquisition, who regarded him as a madman. Gil was a very popular preacher and was designed by Charles V for a bishopric; but it was discovered that some of his sermons in the Cathedral contained unsound propositions regarding such vital doctrines as those of justification by works, the invocation of saints, and purgatory. After proceedings which lasted well over two years he was in August 1552 finally sentenced to abjure ten heretical statements which he admitted he had made. He was confined to the castle of Triana for a year and a number of minor penalties and disabilities were inflicted upon him. Considering the nature of the errors to which he confessed, he was treated with great moderation. Four years after his death a more serious view of his offence was taken, and his bones were exhumed and burnt.

It was not till a little after Egidio's death that the ecclesiastical authorities began to be gravely concerned by the spread of Protestantism in Spain. So far less than a hundred cases in all had been brought before the Inquisition, and in the considerable majority of these foreigners had been involved. Protestantism among natives of the country had appeared to be negligible. But just after Egidio's death suspicions began to be entertained concerning the orthodoxy of the man who had succeeded him in the vacant canonry in Seville Cathedral, by name Constantino Ponce de la Fuente, a former chaplain and confessor to Charles V. Manuscripts of his writing, in which purgatory was

137

described as a bugbear invented by monks to fill their bellies, were discovered together with a store of books by Calvin during a search conducted in the house of a certain widow Isabella Martínez. It was also found at this time that Protestant propagandist works printed at Geneva and Antwerp, some of them by Pérez de Pineda, were finding their way into Seville, as they also were into Valladolid. They were brought into Spain by Julianillo Hernández, a most intrepid reformer who, disguised as a muleteer, smuggled them across the frontier in bales of merchandise.

The little company of Protestants in Seville had as their leaders Ponce de la Fuente and a man of rank by name Juan Ponce de Leon, services being conducted in the house of the latter. Ponce de Leon was kept in confinement for two years. He appears not to have believed that anything more serious would happen to a man of his birth, and was therefore amazed to learn that he was to be burnt. He recanted, and, although this did not save him from the *brasero*, he addressed exhortations to repentance to the other seventeen Lutherans who were relaxed at the great *auto* of September 24, 1559, which attracted thousands of people into the city. Twenty-one other persons accused of Protestantism either made formal abjuration or were reconciled.

At a further *auto* of December 22, 1560, there were fourteen relaxations in person and three in effigy, the latter being of Egidio, Constantino de la Fuente, who had died in prison, and Juan Pérez de Pineda, who was not within the reach of the Inquisition. The most steadfast of those who suffered at this *auto* was Hernández, who had refused to betray his associates in spite of the most dreadful tortures, and who told the friars around him as they exhorted him to repentance that in their hearts they believed as he did but through fear of the Inquisition dared not acknowledge it. Among the other persons relaxed were two Englishmen, named Brooks and Burton respectively. The latter was a ship's captain. All the merchandise on board his vessel was forfeited, and, when another Englishman, named Frampton, was sent out to endeavour to recover the property he not only failed in his mission, but fell into the hands of the Inquisition. As the result of severe torture he promised to embrace Roman Catholicism. He was imprisoned for a year and ordered never to leave Spain.[1]

Two other *autos* were celebrated in Seville in 1562, nine Lutherans being relaxed in person on each occasion. At the second *auto* the crew of a foreign trading vessel appeared, three of them being burnt. Subsequent *autos* in 1564 and 1565 show much reduced numbers, and the majority of the prisoners were foreigners. Indeed at one of them all the six prisoners relaxed were Flemings. It was evident that the small coterie of native Protestants in southern Spain was already obliterated.

Concurrently with the persecution of the Lutherans of Seville there proceeded a similar rooting-out of the little group in northern Spain, whose centre was Valladolid. The founder of this branch was an Italian, named de Seso, who came into Spain armed with a number of heretical books and determined to spread reformed doctrines in the country. He made converts, first, in Logroño in Navarre and then in Valladolid and its neighbourhood. Among the most outstanding of these were Antonio de Herrezuelo, a favourite

[1] Frampton's story is told in Strype's *Annals of the Reformation* (1824), Vol. I, p. 357.

preacher of Charles V named Agustin de Cazalla, his brother Pedro, a parish priest, and the latter's sacristan, Juan Sánchez. Another convert was a Dominican friar named Domingo de Rojas, who won over two other members of his noble family, Pedro Sarmiento and Luis de Rojas. It is probable that this northern group of reformers was not above fifty or sixty in number; they were widely separated, and they had no organization.

Some unguarded talk on the part of one of the converts led to the discovery of the community, if it is permissible so to describe this scattered collection of Protestants, and in the spring of 1558 two denunciations were made to the Inquisition. Sánchez, Domingo de Rojas and de Seso himself, being warned in time, attempted flight. Sánchez was successful, but was caught in the following year. Domingo de Rojas and de Seso reached Pampeluna and seemed to be on the verge of finding security across the Pyrenees when they were recognized.

On Trinity Sunday, May 21, 1559, there took place a great *auto de fe* in Valladolid, at which the two Cazallas and Herrezuelo suffered. Agustin Cazalla had recanted and, like Ponce de Leon at Seville, he was

141

horrified when he learnt that he was to
be put to death. The news did not,
however, affect his now loudly professed
hatred of Protestantism and veneration
for the Holy Office, and on his way to the
brasero he did his utmost to induce the
staunch Herrezuelo to repent. In recognition of his confession Cazalla was gar-
rotted before his body was burnt. The
only prisoner at this *auto* who endured
to the end and was burnt alive was Herrezuelo. He suffered greatly before the
final agony. Gagged that he might not
utter heretical words on his way to the
stake, he was stoned by one of the onlookers and stabbed by one of the soldiers.
Throughout the whole ordeal he never
flinched. His young wife had recanted
and was penanced by perpetual imprisonment. After seven years spent in confinement she withdrew her recantation,
and she was burnt alive in September
1568 as a relapsed heretic. The Valladolid
reformers had been accustomed to hold
services in the house of Cazalla's mother
Leonor de Vibero. She herself had died
before the *auto* of May 21 1559, but her
remains were exhumed and burnt, and
her house was razed to the ground. None
was ever to be erected again on the site

which the Protestant meetings had desecrated. This was in accordance with medieval practice, but there are not many instances of the rule being observed by the Spanish Inquisition. Property was too valuable to be incontinently destroyed.

The remainder of the Valladolid Protestants figured at a second *auto de fe* celebrated in that city on October 8 1559. It was an even greater event than its predecessors, being graced by the presence of Philip II, while there were, it is said, no fewer than 200,000 spectators. Of the twenty-six reformers only two—de Seso and Juan Sánchez—were burnt alive. De Seso had been so severely tortured that he could hardly stand upright to hear his sentence. Domingo de Rojas and Pedro de Cazalla expressed contrition at the *quemadero* and were strangled before their bodies were bound to the stake. There is a familiar story that when de Seso passed in front of the King and asked Philip how he could sanction these horrors, the latter replied : " I myself would bring the wood to burn my own son if he were as perverse as you."

Much the most interesting trial upon the charge of Lutheranism in the history of the Spanish Inquisition is that of

Archbishop Carranza, which has already been discussed in another connection. No notice of the treatment of Protestantism by the Inquisition in the sixteenth century would be complete without some examination of the question whether there was any justification for the proceedings taken against Carranza, or whether these were entirely due to the jealousy of Valdés. The *prima facie* presumption is strongly against one of the greatest dignitaries of the Church in Spain embracing the heresy of the Germans. It is perfectly clear that no one ever had less desire than he to challenge the authority of the Church. If he sinned against the Church he did so unintentionally.

On the other hand, that there were statements in his public utterances and in his writings to which it was possible for an unprejudiced critic to take exception is probably true. It has been suggested that the very fact of Carranza's energetic measures against heresy in England rendered him unduly familiar with erroneous views and liable, perhaps unconsciously, to imbibe them himself. In 1530, long before he attained eminence, he was denounced to the Inquisition as a follower of Erasmus. A man of exemplary life,

144

worthy aims and generous instincts, he was a loose thinker and a confused as well as voluminous writer. His zeal for reform together with his rather undigested opinions, the possible implications of which he was not sufficiently clear-minded to appreciate, rendered it possible to discover in his discursive publications opinions sufficiently akin to Lutheranism, not only to make it possible for his adversaries to make an accusation of heresy appear plausible, but to give genuine cause for perturbation to the severely orthodox. Carranza was alleged to have asserted that Christ had made such complete propitiation for our sins that there was no need for anything on our part save faith in the efficiency of His sacrifice; that all works done without charity are useless and offensive to God; that the human reason does not aid the eye of faith and indeed is prejudicial to it. Such views, which were discovered in the Archbishop's *Commentaries on the Christian Catechism*, were likely to mislead the faithful and to be welcome to the unfaithful. Under torture Domingo de Rojas admitted the influence exerted by that work on the Protestants of Valladolid; and Agustin de Cazalla excused his own errors on the

ground that similar opinions were held
by Carranza. Was it not natural that
grave perturbation should be caused when
the Lutherans of Valladolid could find
warrant for their heresies in the works
of the Archbishop of Toledo himself?
How could the land be protected if heresy
in high places went unreproved? That
is not the whole story. There are cross-
currents in the Carranza case, but there
could have been no Carranza case at all
had there not been plausible means for
making one.

After 1565 native Protestantism in Spain
was practically extinct. In the succeeding centuries native cases are a negligible
factor, while foreigners were frequently
brought before the tribunals. Indeed all
foreigners, especially those coming from
Protestant countries, were apt to be viewed
with suspicion, and seafarers and traders
were in real danger from the Inquisition.
Sometimes the subjects of heretical sovereigns were protected by treaty. Thus in
the Treaty of London (1604), negotiated
between James I of England and Philip III
of Spain, there was an article which stipulated that the subjects of the English
King " should not be molested by land or
sea for matter of conscience, within the

146

King of Spain's . . . dominions, if they gave not occasion of public scandal." Public scandal was defined as failing to make obeisance towards the altar if they entered a church or to bow the knee if they saw the Sacrament being borne through the streets. Similar privileges were obtained by the Dutch in 1609. War, such as broke out between England and Spain in 1624, automatically put an end to this immunity, but it was restored on the conclusion of peace in 1630. The Suprema was careful to point out that it regarded these privileges as appertaining solely to visitors and transient sojourners and that foreigners who were domiciled in the country were as much subject to the jurisdiction of the Holy Office as native Spaniards. It is notorious that negotiations for an Anglo-Spanish alliance carried on between Cromwell and Cardenas, the Spanish ambassador in 1654, broke down because the Protector, not content with the concessions of 1604 and 1630, pressed for liberty of conscience for Englishmen in Spain, for the right to practise their own worship in private houses, as well as for freedom to trade in the Spanish Indies—demands which Cardenas in a famous phrase characterized as asking for his master's two eyes. When Philip III informed the Suprema, in reference to the first of these two proposals, that he would rather risk his kingdom and spill his last drop of blood than do anything to the prejudice of the purity of the faith, the Suprema declared that these words ought to be recorded in imperishable bronze. Subsequent treaties between England and Spain—in 1667, 1713, 1763 and 1783 contained much the same stipulations as those of 1604 and 1630. Protestant minorities in Catholic countries—such as the French Huguenots—did not obtain protection by treaty. In spite of the treaties—and their scope, as we have seen, was limited—there were at all times some foreign Protestants who were liable to be denounced to the Inquisition.[1]

Nevertheless, the importance of Protestantism in the history of the Spanish Inquisition is really confined to the sixteenth century. Lutheranism appeared at a time when the Inquisition seemed to have accomplished its original purpose. The danger apprehended from Moors and

[1] Occasionally a case such as that of Arrowsmith in the seventeenth century or that of Isaac Martin in the eighteenth gained special notoriety and roused great indignation in England.

Marranos had been drastically dealt with ;
the incursion of Portuguese Jews, which
revived persecution for Judaism, had not
yet begun ; and the Holy Office might
have languished from inanition. Valdés
seized the opportunity of imparting fresh
energy to the institution over which he
presided. There is no doubt that the
Lutheran peril had a stimulating effect
upon the Inquisition. Protestants were
regarded with hatred by the great majority
of the population, and of this hostility the
Inquisition took full advantage. It was
represented that there was a serious danger
that the virus of Teutonic heresy might
spread into the Peninsula. In the circumstances the Holy Office received loyal and
enthusiastic support from all classes of
society, from the monarch downwards.
Charles V, whose experience in Germany
led him to regard all heretics as rebels,
characterized them as " seditious, scandalous, violators of the peace, disturbers of
the State." From his retirement in the
Portuguese monastery of S. Juste, he most
earnestly exhorted Philip to punish heretics with all promptitude and severity
and without respect of persons. Philip II
needed no prompting. His slow, bigoted
and conscientious mind was early con-

vinced of the duty and the necessity of pursuing the heretic with relentless piety. Quite sincerely he hated the idea of being ruler of heretic subjects. Balmez, the author of *Protestantism and Catholicity Compared*, honours Philip as the preserver alike of the tranquillity of the Spanish people and of the security of the Spanish monarchy by his resolute support of the Inquisition, which, according to some enthusiastic contemporaries, alone saved Spain from such devastating religious wars as afflicted other countries. By its salutary cauterizings the Inquisition destroyed the cancer which had invaded the healthy body of the nation; like a wall of fire, it preserved the country from the penetration of that plague of irreligion which had overwhelmed Germany.

This is the language of hyperbole, however unconscious the exaggeration may be. Spain was never in any serious danger of Lutheran infection. Even had there been no Inquisition at all it seems unlikely that the Protestant movement would have made any appreciable progress south of the Pyrenees—partly owing to the reform movement among the Spanish clergy, partly because the population, largely as the result of its hatred of Moors and

Jews, had acquired an intense repugnance for all forms of heresy.

The chief significance of the episode of Lutheranism in Spain is that it increased the suspicion felt for all things foreign, the apprehension that danger might lurk in any ideas which were at all novel or venturesome. Carranza blamed the advent of Protestantism for the restrictions which were placed upon the reading of the Scriptures in the vulgar tongue; there was, he said, no such restraint " before the heresies of the accursed Luther came from hell to the light of day." And indeed the interest of the Inquisition in the censorship of books dates from the Lutheran scare. But to blame Luther for the censorship of the Press was as illogical as it was characteristic of the inquisitor's mentality. The occasional abuse of liberty does not justify its permanent repression.

151

CHAPTER VII

MYSTICS

THE spiritual soil of Spain was not conducive to the growth of Protestantism, but there are certain aberrations of Mysticism which bear some resemblance to Protestantism, and Mysticism was a spontaneous development of the religious fervour of the Spaniard. While Mysticism has been found to be perfectly compatible with the strictest orthodoxy, and many great mystics figure among the saints of the Catholic Church, it has shown an inherent tendency to generate extravagances both of thought and conduct. The problems arising from this proclivity provided the Spanish Inquisition with a large variety of cases—many of them difficult—spread over the greater part of its existence. The boundary line between orthodox and heretical Mysticism is perplexing and difficult to define, and it is not surprising that the greatest of Spanish mystics, even those who died in all the odour of sanctity, including some who have been beatified or even canonized, were at one time or another suspected of heresy, while some of them were arraigned before the Holy Office.

The essential concept of Mysticism is that the soul can by complete self-surrender, complete abstraction from mundane things and absorbed contemplation of the Godhead, pass into a spiritual apprehension of divine truth beyond the powers of the understanding. The idea is by no means confined to Christianity, and is found nowhere more potently than in Hinduism. Wherever it is found it arises from the conviction that the mystery of the divine nature is such that the human intellect unaided cannot attain to the knowledge of it, but that God can impart to those who yearn for Him a capacity for comprehension which is independent of the reason. What is needed to allow of the inflowing of the spirit of God into the human heart is openness to receive it; and that openness will come if there is intense desire for Him. To the Christian mystics no virtue is comparable with love. The love of God, if it be a genuine passion and not a mere sentiment, can, like human love, find satisfaction only in union with the One beloved, and those who earnestly seek such spiritual fellowship will at least in measure find fulfilment.

Certain fundamental doctrines of the Christian religion are essentially mystical —the incarnation, the indwelling of the Holy Ghost, communion through the sacraments. Yet in every age of the Church there have been mystics who have met with reprobation. The mysticism of the author of the Fourth Gospel and of St. Paul is one thing; that of the Gnostics another. In the Middle Ages the mysticism of Hugo of St. Victor, of St. Francis, of Bonaventura, of Joachim of Flora, even of John Tauler was approved; but that of Amaury de Bène and of Master Eckhart, Tauler's master, was condemned. The soul filled with the divine illumination of the Holy Ghost, even if it commit sin, is blameless, taught Amaury; while Eckhart, proclaiming the pantheist doctrine of the common divinity of God and man, asserted that in God's sight there is no difference between good and evil. These pantheist and antinomian ideas were condemned by the Church, and the Beghards and other disciples of the illuminist gospel were persecuted as heretics.

Mystic experience is essentially personal

experience; it means direct contact between the individual soul and God. It is not surprising, therefore, that some mystics should make light of the functions of the priesthood as mediators between man and God. The observance of the services of the Church, said Juan de la Cruz, one of the greatest of Spanish mystics and poets, and the use of images, and even of places of worship, is intended only for the uninitiated. Such things may be likened to the toys of childhood. Those who have advanced in the religious life have no further need of them. Such doctrines are suggestive of the Protestant insistence on the inwardness of religion, of the necessity of salvation by faith, of the unimportance of form and ceremony.[1] Some of the Spanish mystics came very close to Lutheranism. The inquisitors recognized three types of mystics who were to be reckoned as heretics. There were, first, the *alumbrados* or illuminists, who dwelt upon the supreme efficacy of the inward light and who were contemptuous of ecclesiastical authority and priestly

[1] P. S. Rodriguez, in his *Introducción á la Historia de la Literatura Mística en España* (Madrid, 1927), divides the heterodox mystics into three classes— Protestant, pantheist, and quietist.

instruction. There were, in the second place, the *dejados* or quietists, who, annihilating themselves in abandonment to God, allowed free course to every idea and every impulse which came to them during their trances or meditations. Lastly, there were the impostors who made profit out of the impious simulation of mystic sanctity and of spiritual gifts, which deceived the credulous.

It is clear that the visionary ecstasies and the extremes of self-abasement, which go with certain types of Mysticism, made the same strong appeal to the pious Spaniard that the austerities or self-torture of the yogi make to the pious Hindu. The mystic idea is romantic and Spain is a land of romance. Its literature is full of the ideas of chivalry—of the quest of a superhuman ideal, of the redemption of the sinner by extraordinary devotion to the Virgin, and of similar themes. There is something very fine and very beautiful in the semi-heroic, semi-ascetic conception of the religious life. But such romanticism may occasionally degenerate into mere sentimentality. A still worse type of debasement is sometimes met with—morbid, unwholesome, pathological. The unhealthy extravagances to which *dejamiénto* could go are well illustrated by the story, recounted by Southey in his *Letters from Spain and Portugal,* of the career of Dona Luisa de Carvajal y Mendoza, who after a terrible upbringing, during which she was continually beaten with a whip of catgut, submitting to the humiliations and barbarities inflicted upon her with complete resignation, obtained great celebrity by her practices of sleeping on planks, wearing horsecloth next her skin, bracelets of bristles, a wooden cross made with spikes upon her breast, and another made like a sort of nutmeg-grater between her shoulders. Worse than delight in, and admiration for, self-inflicted torments was mere sexual depravity, either induced by mystical antinomianism or, perhaps more often, hypocritically ascribed to that source by those who indulged in it.

Some of the abnormalities of Mysticism, when they were brought to the notice of inquisitors, presented no difficulty—when, for example, their fruits were manifest corruption, or when the doctrine was taught that if an unholy thought was suggested to the mind during prayer or mystic abstraction it ought immediately to be put into execution. But even the most virtuous and indeed most saintly of mystics were liable to arouse suspicion, and the Inquisition did not always find it easy to decide upon the border-line between what was safe and what was dangerous. Even Santa Theresa herself, the greatest and most lovable of all Spanish mystics, though there was little doctrine in her visionary and ascetic, yet practical, faith, was at one time in danger of being prosecuted, and when her spiritual autobiography appeared in 1575 it was denounced to the Inquisition, which took ten years to decide whether it was right for the faithful to read it. Her *Conceptos del Amor Divino* was placed on the Index. Juan of Avila, a great preacher, the apostle of Andalusia, was brought before the Inquisition in 1534. But Manrique personally intervened, and he was accorded a triumphal vindication, being welcomed, when he reappeared in the pulpit, by a fanfare of trumpets. Juan de la Cruz was more than once denounced as an *alumbrado*, to the tribunals of Valladolid, Toledo and Seville. Luis of Granada's work, *Guia de Pecadores*, one of the classics of Spanish Mysticism, was placed upon the Index, though this prohibition was soon removed. Luis de Leon, whose story can be more appropriately dealt with in another connection, famous both as mystic and humanist, had to justify himself before the Holy Office. A number of the early Jesuits, including Ignatius Loyola himself, were suspected of being illuminists. Certain of the Dominicans—notably Melchor Cano and one named Alonso de la Fuente—hostile to the new Company of Jesus, asserted that its members were all *alumbrados*. The latter, as the result of protracted independent investigations in the 1570's, which he carried out in the Estremadura, persuaded himself that that region harboured a widespread sect of illuminists, whose persuasion could be traced to the influence of one single Jesuit. He tried to arouse the Suprema to a proper appreciation of the danger. The Council at first found little or nothing to justify de la Fuente's alarms, but the local tribunal at Llerena became busy and at last at an *auto* held in June 1579 fifteen *alumbrados* appeared. However, the penalties inflicted were not very heavy, and the arrest of but fifteen culprits afforded little justification for the lurid tales of the corrupt mysticism of the Jesuits.

If there were proved to have been malpractices among few of the mystics of the Estremadura, there was little or no unorthodoxy. It had been otherwise among a band of mystics who were found rather earlier in the century at Guadalajara. One of their preachers, a layman named Ruiz de Alcaraz, was accused of teaching that mental prayer alone was needed, that sexual union was union with God, and denying the efficacy of confession, indulgences and good works. He was severely tortured and confessed. He had incurred the penalty of relaxation, but was sentenced to perpetual imprisonment, confiscation and to flogging in Guadalajara and other places in which he had preached. One or two members of the Guadalajara group were accused of being Lutherans as well as illuminists.

Mystic ideas, if pushed to extremes, were, as inquisitors found by experience, apt to lead to very dangerous tenets. A work on spiritual discipline and mental prayer written by an obscure priest, together with a number of miscellaneous papers by the same author, when submitted to inquisitorial censors, was declared to be full of doctrinal errors of varying magnitude, including some very heretical propositions, such as the licentious doctrine that the perfect soul has entire liberty exempt from every kind of law. Devotion to the use of images, rosaries, etc., was denounced as so dangerous that it precluded all hope of salvation. In January 1578 the Suprema added to the Edict of Faith a list of illuminist errors for the information of the faithful. Among the propositions enumerated was the disparagement of liturgical prayer on the ground that inward prayer alone was necessary, the derision of the use of images and other aids to devotion and of good works, since the perfect had no need to perform them. A much longer list of illuminist errors was issued in an Edict of Grace of May 1623 by order of the Inquisitor-general Pacheco in consequence of revelations of indecencies which were being practised under the name of mystic ecstasies through the influence of a fanatical or demented priest in Seville. It is worth noting that the list was criticized upon the ground that it included, together with a number of undoubted heresies, propositions which were quite unexceptionable, indeed the accepted teaching of the Church.

Thirty days were allowed for the guilty in Seville in which to denounce themselves. It appears that it came as a terrible shock to many citizens, both rich and poor, to discover that they had laid themselves open to the suspicion of heresy; their one idea was to clear themselves at the first opportunity from a reproach which horrified them. Hundreds presented themselves and the inquisitor on duty had to remain from early morning till late at night listening to their self-incriminations. They had been guilty of foolishness; some of them very likely of conduct that was worse than foolish. They had been carried away by the extravagances of a man whose megalomania suggests insanity; they had been misled into accepting his reputation for marvellous sanctity. Not one of them had been guilty of the sin of heresy. There were subsequent cases of Illuminism in Seville. Sometimes numerous errors were imputed to the culprits, but after a while the Inquisition treated these as aberrations in morals, not in doctrine.

It continued to do so prior to the excitement created by the teachings of by far the most celebrated of Spain's heretic mystics, Miguel de Molinos. The Mysticism of Molinos knew nothing of the ecstasies and the visions of Santa Theresa; he was the arch-priest of *dejamiénto*, of the conception that by annihilating the outward world of sense the soul may attain to that perfect silence in which the word of God can be heard. It was in Rome that Molinos made his great reputation as teacher and confessor and as the author of the *Guia Espirituale*. For a considerable time he was safe in the protection of Innocent XI, but criticism was aroused when it was found that his followers abandoned the use of their rosaries and while absorbed in silent prayer would entirely ignore the elevation of the Host. The Jesuits, at an earlier date themselves suspected of mystic errors, ranged themselves against Molinos, and secured the help of Père La Chaise, the confessor to Louis XIV, who brought influence to bear upon that monarch. In November 1685 the Spanish Inquisition condemned the *Guia Espirituale* as containing illuminist heresies. In the same month the Congregation of the Roman Inquisition, acting on the representations of the French ambassador, arrested Molinos, and nearly three years later found him guilty of a great many heretical, erroneous or blasphemous views. He remained in prison until his death in 1696. After this the term Molinist came to supplant that of *alumbrado* in the vocabulary of

163

the Spanish Inquisition, and it was often used to designate one who persuaded himself, or pretended to persuade himself, that in the condition of *dejamiénto* he might freely indulge his passions and yet remain impeccable. Down to about the middle of the eighteenth century cases of Molinism continued to be brought before the tribunal of the Inquisition, especially in the north of Spain. In the latter years of the century the Holy Office tended to attribute self-denunciation for this crime and claims to abnormal spiritual powers to delusion or insanity, and it was probably right in nearly every case in taking this charitable view.

The movement produced a considerable crop of impostors, especially among women, both in the sixteenth and seventeenth centuries. Such in all probability was Francisca Hernández, who gained such a reputation for holiness of life that when Adrian of Utrecht became pope he besought her prayers for himself and the Catholic Church. She spoke of herself as a bride of Christ and her followers claimed that she was so deeply filled with the Holy Ghost as to be impeccable. She plainly exercised great fascination over some men, and ugly stories were bruited

164

abroad as to her true relations with them. She was twice arrested, but it appears that nothing was ever brought home against her. But about her more famous contemporary Magdalena de la Cruz there was eventually no such hesitation. Her reputation for holiness and for prophetic powers spread far beyond the boundaries of Spain, and both secular princes and princes of the Church asked for her advice, her prayers and her blessings. But when she fell desperately ill in 1543, being in fear of death, she voluntarily confessed that her visions and her prophecies had all been due to demoniacal possession, and that she had been visited by a familiar spirit who came to her in the guise of an Adonis. She recovered and was at once brought before the Inquisition. The reading of the catalogue of her offences at the *auto de fe*, at which she appeared in May 1546, lasted eight hours.

There are a good many similar cases. Here is a certain Maria de la Visitacion of Lisbon whose holiness is such that she claims to possess the stigmata of Christ. She associates herself with the movement for securing the independence of Portugal from Spain, and in 1588 proceedings are taken against her. Soap and water entirely remove the stigmata. She is sentenced to be whipped twice every week, to take her meals always on the floor of her convent and to lie down in the doorway of the refectory so that the nuns may trample upon her as they leave. Another nun, who lays claim to great holiness and to marvellous ecstasies, is eventually declared to harbour all the errors of the Mohammedans, Nestorians, Lutherans, Calvinists and Illuminists. Another, having asserted that she has been able to liberate millions of souls from purgatory, is found to be an obdurate heretic, and she is sentenced to relaxation. Her blasphemies on the way to the stake are so horrible that she has to be gagged. Another, who like the rest has had ecstatic visions and has worked miracles, being possessed of magic cures for the pains of childbirth and for many diseases, dies under torture but not before she has confessed herself an impostor.

Mysticism was one of the great religious movements of the sixteenth century. It was a manifestation of a genuine religious revival; it was also in part an emotional reaction against rigidity of doctrine and formalism of religious practice. It was a powerful factor in the Counter-Reformation; it produced Santa Theresa, Juan de la Cruz, Luis of Granada in Spain; Molinos in Italy; Madame Guyon and Fénelon in France. It has its pictorial representation in El Greco. Because it was emotional it was apt to pass the bounds of reason occasionally. It sometimes gave rise to an unhealthy eroticism; in weak intellects it produced the wildest delusions; in weaklings of another kind it excited indecency and immorality. It afforded too easy an opportunity to the mere charlatan. Llorente considers that the Inquisition was excellently employed in flogging the nonsense out of the weaklings and the wickedness out of the rogues, and only regrets that it did not confine its activities to so useful and admirable a task.

CHAPTER VIII

MISCELLANEOUS ACTIVITIES OF THE INQUISITION

THE Inquisition dealt with a great many offences besides those which have so far been discussed. We have seen that questions concerning forfeited property and its claim to jurisdiction where its own members were concerned brought before it many cases in which no heresy was involved at all. It also tried persons who, while not heretics themselves, were fautors or protectors of heretics or who impeded the tribunals and their ministers in the carrying out of their duties. Pius V in 1569 pronounced the penalties of anathema, deprivation of office and confiscation of property against those who hindered the Inquisition in any way, molested its officers, destroyed its records or aided the escape of its prisoners. The smallest wrong done to one of its servants, complains Llorente, was punished as though it was an offence against religion. The Holy Office was also concerned with offences which, though not directly heretical, were akin to heresy or implied the existence of erroneous doctrines, such as sorcery and witchcraft, bigamy, solicitation in the confessional, and the utterance of pernicious or scandalous opinions. The Holy Office also undertook the censorship of books. This function, together with the prosecution of new types of heresy which arose in the eighteenth century, such as Jansenism, Rationalism and Freemasonry, occupied the Inquisition in its later and less influential days. A brief survey of the more important of the activities just summarized must be attempted even in a brief account of the Spanish Inquisition.

The treatment of reputed wizards and witches forms one of the most interesting chapters in the history of the medieval and modern Inquisitions. Prior to the pontificate of John XXII, an implacable foe of the accursed tribe of magicians, there existed no pronouncement that there was anything necessarily heretical in necromancy. Astrology was much practised in Spain, and vagabonds, mainly Jewish and Moorish women, told fortunes and worked spells for the averting of the evil eye or for the preservation of crops and cattle, without let or hindrance. Eymeric made a distinction between divination by palmistry, which was comparatively harmless and which could be left to the secular courts, and divination by means of the aping of religious ceremonies, which was a matter for trial by the bishops. But soon after the accession of Ferdinand Edicts of Faith came to include the admonition to denounce sorcerers as heretics, and before the end of the sixteenth century the Holy Office was claiming exclusive jurisdiction over them. While difficulty was found in determining when heresy was and when it was not implicit in the use of the black arts, the view came to prevail that there must be at least suspicion of heresy.

Procedure in cases of sorcery differed little from that employed in heresy trials except that there was no use of torture. The penalties inflicted by the Inquisition were much lighter than those in vogue in the secular courts. This does not mean that the Inquisition had any doubts about the authenticity of sorcery ; it was indeed still dealing with the crime at the end of the eighteenth century on the assumption that it implied an actual contract with Satan. A poor man, who having in a state of despair taken the advice of a woman magician and invoked Satan with no result, was imprisoned for denying the existence of the world of darkness. The two most interesting cases of sorcery in the annals of the Spanish Inquisition are those of Froilan Díaz, already mentioned, and of Dr. Torralba, the physician referred to in *Don Quixote*, who perhaps out of sheer vanity claimed to have dealings with a familiar spirit and who paid for his imprudence by a three-years' imprisonment.

In the fifteenth century Europe was seized by a great witchcraft scare. Sprenger in his *Malleus Maleficarum* and Bernard of Como, the great authorities on the subject in that period, who detail the stories of the Sabbat, or midnight concourse with Satan, to which the witches are transported through the air, of their fell influence upon the fruitfulness of the earth and the fruitfulness of man, were apparently convinced that a new danger had suddenly afflicted Christendom. Reputed witches were subjected to terrible torture, Sprenger and others having taught that obduracy and taciturnity under torment were sure signs of demoniacal aid. It is now generally accepted that delusion, madness and torture were the three be-

171   M

getters of practically all the evidence for witchcraft.

The isolation of Spain from the rest of Europe preserved it from the witchcraft scare until the very end of the fifteenth century, and it is significant that when it did come, it was almost confined to Navarre, which was in the extreme north and inhabited by an ignorant peasantry. In consequence of the alleged outbreak of a plague of witches the Suprema in 1526 appointed a committee of ten members to discuss the question, Valdés being its most prominent member. The majority came to the conclusion that the evidence forthcoming was quite inadequate, and that the crimes attributed to the supposed witches were probably delusions. At a time when in other European countries witches were generally credited with the power of producing sterility and with the habits of vampires, and burnt for these iniquities, this committee decided that witches who were charged with compassing people's deaths and sucking the blood of infants ought not to be handed over to the secular arm as murderers, because there was nothing to prove that any murders had actually been committed. They were agreed that the Inquisition was a proper body to take cognizance of alleged cases of witchcraft, but believing that prevention was better than cure, they came to the conclusion that the first step to take was the sending out of preachers to enlighten the ignorant populace. The inquisitor of Navarre, however, was not deterred from finding a large number of witches among the mountains, and he appears to have brought some fifty women or more to their deaths, being satisfied in his own mind of the veracity of the stories of the Sabbat and the other abominations imputed to them.

The Suprema maintained its own attitude of caution and scepticism, pointing out to tribunals the extreme difficulties presented by the stories of witchcraft and laying emphasis on the need of careful verification of all the evidence. Inquisitors were reminded that they must not take everything which they found in the *Malleus Maleficarum* for gospel : which was precisely what inquisitors in other countries were doing. When complaints were made that the Holy Office was treating the crime of witchcraft with improper clemency, the Suprema simply deprecated the severity with which reputed witches were dealt with in the secular courts, and pointed out that the whole question was much more intricate than the complainants seemed to imagine.

For the space of about seventy-five years the Suprema consistently maintained its eminently moderate and enlightened attitude, doing its utmost to combat the credulity of the multitude and to mitigate the indiscreet zeal of some of the tribunals. In 1610 there was a temporary setback, the members of the Council at that date being apparently scared out of their disbelief by the sheer mass of evidence which was hurled upon them from Navarre. It really did seem as though Satan was very busy in those parts, and that the local inquisitors were right in bestirring themselves against him.

Less remarkable than the setback itself was its immediate consequence. Next spring the Suprema dispatched into Navarre a special inquisitor, Alonso de Salazar Frias, whose name deserves to be held in lasting honour. His coming appears to have created great alarm, for when an Edict of Grace was published hundreds of persons came forward to accuse themselves of nefarious dealings with the Evil one. The great majority of them were mere children. Salazar came to the conclusion that at least three-quarters of these self-incriminators had committed perjury, and that there was no evidence of witchcraft whatsoever. He maintained that in the existing state of the public mind in Navarre Edicts of Grace simply nourished the evil. There had been no witches until they were written and talked about. The Suprema, strengthened by Salazar's report, resumed its former attitude, and insisted once again upon the necessity of a real sifting of evidence and of preachers explaining to their flocks that children died suddenly and crops failed in countries where there were no witches at all and that natural phenomena, such as disease and bad weather, were generally the causes of such calamities. After 1610 few witchcraft trials figure in the annals of the Inquisition, and there are none at all in the eighteenth century.

While the Suprema never categorically denied the possibility of there being women possessed of supernatural powers due to a compact with the Devil, and indeed kept an open mind on the subject, it did its best to insist upon the necessity of objective evidence and to discourage mere superstition. The story of its attitude to witchcraft forms indeed the most honourable chapter in the annals of the Spanish Inquisition.

The crime of bigamy was normally tried in the episcopal courts, but the Inquisition frequently met with it in dealing with the Moriscos, any lapse from strict monogamy being suggestive of relapse into Mohammedanism, and ere long it tended to usurp the jurisdiction of the diocesan. The offence came within the purview of the Holy Office only when it indicated the existence of erroneous beliefs regarding the sacrament of marriage, but it was not difficult to argue that it invariably did so unless the sin was committed in ignorance, when there was valid reason for supposing that the first wife or husband was dead. The secular as well as the ecclesiastical courts claimed jurisdiction over bigamy, and in the eighteenth century, under Charles III, an uneasy tripartite division of authority was arranged whereby legal questions such as that of the legitimacy of offspring was apportioned to the secular court, that of the validity of the marriage to the episcopal court, that of the heresy involved to the Inquisition. But this arrangement proved impracticable, and the Inquisition did most of the work. The cases of bigamy with which it dealt were very numerous. The records of the tribunal of Toledo in the seventeenth and eighteenth centuries show them to stand second in order of frequency.

The unsavoury subject of solicitation in the confessional may be passed over lightly, but it is impossible to ignore it altogether since it bulked largely in the business of the inquisitorial tribunals. The scandal of priests using the confessional for the seduction of their female penitents was normally one for the diocesan courts to deal with, but, as with bigamy, so with this offence, the Holy Office tended to demand exclusive jurisdiction, on the ground that a priest could hardly commit this sin without having very erroneous notions indeed about the sacrament of confession. Paul IV and several of his successors definitely called upon inquisitors to take this matter in hand, although some people deprecated calling attention to such a scandal because publicity would discourage the practice of confession and encourage the Lutherans. There were inherent difficulties in dealing with such cases. In the nature of things the only evidence forthcoming must be that of the complainant; there could be no corrobor-

177

ative testimony. That being so, it was necessary to guard against the possibilities of mere slander, and the inquisitors had to be guided to a great extent by what they knew of the characters and reputations of the informant and of the alleged offender respectively. The word of a woman of notoriously bad character could not be accepted against a priest who had always lived a blameless life. On the other hand, the accusation of a woman of modest and sensitive character, who would be naturally reluctant to face the ordeal of the inquisitor's interrogatory unless she had urgent cause, was usually accepted.

The Inquisition's treatment of the crime of solicitation was not very satisfactory. It would have been better left to the bishops, to be dealt with in accordance with the moral turpitude involved. The Inquisition, considering the doctrinal and not the ethical aspect, inflicted only light penalties—usually abjuration *de levi* in private, perpetual deprivation of the right to hear confessions, and some spiritual penance. Moreover, the inquisitorial definition of the crime was exceedingly technical. If the solicitation took place before or after confession : if the penitent came to confess, but the confession was post-

178

poned, then, however improper the priest's conduct, there was no abuse of the sacrament and consequently no doctrinal error. It followed also from the Inquisition's attitude to the offence, that the excuse that the sin had been committed under the stress of sudden impulse constituted a mitigation of the heinousness of the act. The point of view adopted by the Holy Office was perfectly consistent with its proper functions, but this only shows that it was not the appropriate body to deal with a crime the essential evil of which was moral, not intellectual. We are told that when the edict calling for denunciation of confessors who had been guilty of solicitation was first published in Seville in 1563, there came such a rush of women to lodge information that the notaries could not cope with the situation and it was necessary to extend the period for receiving accusations by a whole month. As the authority for this tale was not in Spain but in Germany at the time it is probably a great exaggeration; but certainly solicitation is one of the offences which most frequently figures in inquisitorial records.

Other offences against morals with which heretical intent could be read were the contracting of marriage by one in Holy

179

orders in defiance of the rule of celibacy, which the Council of Trent declared to be heretical, unnatural crime and blasphemy. A word may be said in passing about blasphemy. Some of the expletives commonly used in Spain certainly had an heretical sound—for example, " Pese á Dios ! " (May God repent !) and " Reniego á Dios " (I renounce God) ; but as they were used in anger or vexation thoughtlessly, and as the secular law contained adequate penalties for the offence, inquisitors usually felt that they could leave blasphemy to be dealt with by other authorities and concentrate their own attention on more important things. But latterly when the number of serious cases of heresy decreased the use of such an oath as " Reniego á Dios " was sometimes punished as heretical.

One species of unseemly conduct with which the Inquisition was greatly concerned was that of rash, thoughtless or scandalous conversation about sacred things.[1] Simancas observes that it is

[1] The proposition that fornication between unmarried persons is not a mortal sin was very frequently punished by the Inquisition, and with severity—abjuration *de levi* with scourging or *vergüenza* being the normal penalties.

unsafe even for the wisest and most learned to dispute concerning controversial topics of faith and religion. It is therefore prudent for a writer or speaker, if he must needs discuss such things, to preface what he has to say by stating that he has no intention of deviating from the Catholic faith in any particular but entirely embraces it, so as to make it quite clear that if he errs he does so in ignorance and not in malice. Such a protestation, the bishop adds, would not save one who voluntarily erred, even were it repeated a thousand times. A system which was designed to secure the utmost circumspection in the casual conversation of the ordinary man or woman created difficulties for the preacher and the teacher. The former was liable to find himself informed against by the most ignorant of his auditors for any statement which sounded strange or objectionable to them. In such circumstances originality became dangerous. " The risks of the Christian preacher are no small matter," it was said. " If the inquisitors proceeded against all those who are denounced to them, there would not be found a single preacher of the word of God."

Adventurous thinkers were always in

danger of being brought before the Inquisition on the score of statements and opinions which gave offence to less nimble or more conventional minds. Luis de Leon was one of the most attractive and one of the most brilliant Spaniards of the sixteenth century. He has been described as " a Castilian blend of Milton, Wordsworth, and Savonarola." [1] In the dialectical contests which frequently took place in the University of Salamanca, of which he was a professor, he was often triumphantly engaged, and in consequence he made enemies. The University was occupied in editing a new edition of the Latin Bible. Luis, who was a Converso by descent, was accused of showing insufficient respect for the text of the Vulgate, in whose verbal inspiration he did not believe, being conscious of the numerous errors which had crept into it. He had also translated the *Song of Solomon* into Castilian with a commentary in which the book was treated more as a love poem than as an allegory. On these accounts Luis de Leon was denounced to the Inquisition. He was treated with leniency in view of his age and frailties. He identified several of the enemies who had

[1] A. V. G. Bell, *Luis de Leon* (1925), p. 11.

testified against him and made a masterly
defence. But the trial went on and on
and the *calificadores* pronounced that he
had merely multiplied his errors in his
attempt to excuse them. Eventually the
tribunal failed to agree, and the case was
referred to the Suprema, which in December 1576 acquitted Luis, but reprimanded
him and warned him to treat theological
questions with more caution in future.

But caution was foreign to the nature
of this ardent scholar, poet and mystic.
Once more in 1582 he became involved in
a controversy in his University in defence
of the doctrines of a Jesuit named Monte-
mayor on the subject of free will and
predestination against a Dominican friar.
This led on to debates on other highly
contentious questions. Once more Luis
was denounced to the Inquisition; once
more the proceedings were very protracted;
once more he was reprimanded—this time
by Quiroga, the Inquisitor-general himself,
whose personal friendship seems to have
saved him worse humiliations.[1]

[1] Once, after his return to the University of
Salamanca, when he was asked by a student, he
replied: " I am hoarse. Besides, it is better to
speak low, so that the gentlemen of the Inquisition
may not hear."

Similar to the case of Luis de Leon is that of another professor at Salamanca, Francisco Sánchez, better known, from his birthplace las Brozas, as El Brocense. Intellectually arrogant, and utterly contemptuous of dull-witted folk, this fine scholar made trouble for himself by his love of paradox, his recklessness of speech, and his special scorn of theologians. Among his *obiter dicta* in the lecture-room, which caused offence among some of his auditors, were the statements that Christ was born, not in December but in September, not in a manger but in a house, that He was circumcised not by St. Simeon but by the Virgin, that saints in heaven were to be adored but not images, which were but wood and plaster. These propositions were regarded as heretical by the local tribunal, but the Suprema knew Sánchez well by reputation and were not disposed towards severity. Before the Suprema he defended himself with the most robust vigour, justifying everything he had said. Eventually he was reprimanded and warned, just as Luis de Leon had been. But in his classroom the old freedom of speech was soon heard as of yore, and two of the volumes he subsequently published were full of his mali-

184

cious contempt for theologians. He was summoned before the Inquisition once again—in 1600, but he was mildly treated and allowed to keep prison in the house of his son, a physician of Valladolid. The attitude of the Inquisition on both occasions was that there was nothing worthy of really serious censure in what Sánchez had actually said, but that he was too arrogant and presumptuous. They considered him a mere grammarian, so puffed up with secular learning that he imagined himself to be qualified to lay down the law on all subjects. In a pathetic appeal to the inquisitors written when he knew himself to be dying, El Brocense protested his adherence in all particulars to the Catholic faith, declaring that he had never written a book without commending his work to God. If, considering the outspokenness of Sánchez's language, it is remarkable that the Inquisition should have shown such forbearance towards him, it is still more worthy of note that with the inquisitorial system in existence it was difficult for men of exuberant minds to avoid molestation, and that persons of less courage or greater prudence than Luis de Leon and Sánchez held their peace even when the scholar's

185

zest or a sense of humour provoked to speech.

In the eighteenth century, in the days of its decadence, the Inquisition was very largely occupied with combating what seemed obnoxious in the work of a scholar, the writer and the philosopher. There were one or two new heresies to be kept at bay. Jansenism, which had its birth in the Netherlands, and which was a powerful and distracting force in France during the second half of the reign of Louis XIV, was never powerful in Spain : still there were a few Jansenists, and the Jesuits, the arch-enemies of Jansenism, were very influential with the Inquisition. Even after the hostility of the Jesuits to the policy of Charles III led to their expulsion from the kingdom in 1767, the Inquisition continued to endeavour to suppress Jansenist opinions. There was also Free-masonry, which Clement XII in 1738 condemned as a most pernicious thing, to be eradicated by the united efforts of bishops and inquisitors. Few lodges were founded in Spain before 1760, but after that, with the personal help of Cagliostro, the movement made headway. When it developed a revolutionary character its members were dealt with by the secular authorities, but, particularly in the last few years of its existence, after the restoration of 1814, the Inquisition showed some vigour against Free-masonry.[1] But the new phenomenon which the Inquisition held most thoroughly in detestation in the age of enlightenment was the kind of philosophy which emanated from France. The French thinkers differed much among themselves, but they were alike in being a very subversive influence, and many of them, if they were not actually critical of Christianity itself, were hostile to the Catholic Church. Their views were anathema, not only to the Inquisition, but to the vast majority of the Spanish people, and it was but a feeble echo of the new intellectual movement that penetrated south of the Pyrenees. On the other hand, some cultured Spaniards who travelled abroad became interested in the ideas of the *éclaircissement*.

Such was a young and aspiring lawyer, Pablo Olavide, who made the personal

[1] They were sometimes regarded as a species of Manichæans. Cf. a pamphlet of 1752, " Verdadera Cronologia de los Maniqueos que aun existen con el nombre de Franc-masones." See V. de la Fuente, *Historia de las Sociedades secretas . . . en España* (Vol. III, 1871), pp. 422–8.

acquaintance of both Rousseau and Voltaire when in France, and corresponded with them upon his return to Spain. He was denounced to the Inquisition as an atheist, who disbelieved in miracles and in the exclusive salvation of Catholics. Many witnesses appeared against him and scores of heretical propositions were attributed to him. After he had already spent two years in prison he was in November 1778 found guilty, and sentenced to. eight years' confinement in a convent, confiscation of property and civic disabilities, which were to affect four generations of his descendants. In an earlier period he would undoubtedly have been burnt, but even this much milder punishment was so much out of accord with the spirit of the age in other countries that it brought great odium upon the Inquisition. Olavide succeeded in escaping from Spain in 1780. Eighteen years later he published so moving an account of his disillusionment as a philosopher and of his contrition as a Catholic that he was allowed to return to his own country.

The Holy Office was not the power that it had been of yore. Some of those most strongly suspected of being free-thinkers were in high places—such as Charles III's minister, the Conde de Aranda. In its great days it had not hesitated to strike at officers of state, and it could usually count upon the sovereign's support in doing so. But it was different now ; royal favour could not invariably be relied upon. Certainly Charles III's adviser was beyond attack. However, in 1789 Charles IV, very much alarmed at the trend of. affairs in France, came to the conclusion that all revolutionary principles were heretical *per se*, and the Inquisition, promptly acting upon this view, ordered that all French newspapers coming into the country should be delivered to its officers. But the task of keeping French ideas entirely at bay proved to be beyond the united powers of Crown and Inquisition, and even Spain had its revolution in 1812.

It was only natural that an institution whose function was the protection of the faithful from the contagion of error should be concerned with the superintendence of the Press. The invention of printing made the dissemination of false doctrine easier than ever before. Alexander VI in 1501 called upon the German bishops to deal with the abuses of the new art which had **its** birth in that country. A Lateran

Council in 1515 laid it down that no book should be printed save after examination by the proper ecclesiastical authority. In 1502 Ferdinand and Isabella ordered that no book should be printed, imported, or sold without preliminary licence. So far there was no mention of the Inquisition. Torquemada at an *auto* in 1490 had publicly burnt 600 volumes which contained Judaist and other heresies, but it was not till 1521 that, following an appeal from Leo X to the Spanish authorities to prevent the introduction of Lutheran writings into their country, Adrian of Utrecht issued an edict that prohibited books should be brought to the inquisitors in order that they might be publicly burnt. In 1536 the Suprema decided to act as a licensing authority, but in 1550 it thought better of this and henceforward was content with the condemnation of bad books, leaving the approval of good ones to others.

The denunciation of printed works which appeared to him to contain matter injurious to the faith was now imposed as one of the duties of the good Catholic in the Edicts of Faith, and any book of which complaint was made was submitted to *calificadores*, who reported to the Suprema their recommendation of no action, prohibition or expurgation as the case might be. Persons in possession of a work condemned by the Suprema on the advice of its experts had to bring it in either for destruction or for the obliteration of offending passages. This system obviously necessitated the drawing up of lists of prohibited books. The first such list was compiled, at the request of Charles V, by the University of Louvain in 1546. In 1551 the Spanish Inquisition issued a new edition of this with an extra list of some books in Castilian and in Latin compiled by itself. After the discovery of the extensive smuggling of Lutheran literature by Hernández, Valdés decided that the Spanish Inquisition should undertake the production of an *Index Librorum Prohibitorum* entirely its own. This big enterprise—Francisco Sánchez was among those employed in it—was completed in 1559. Between this Spanish Index and the more famous Tridentine or Papal Index, which appeared in 1564, there was the notable difference that whereas the latter made no distinction between works objectionable in their entirety and those which were objectionable only in part, the former discriminated

between those which were definitely condemned and others which were sanctioned
on condition that the offending passages
were expunged.

Lists of books soon grow out of date,
and it was not long before it was deemed
necessary to issue a new Index. The
work, which was entrusted to the University of Salamanca, took several years.
At last in 1583 and 1584 respectively
there were issued two volumes, one a list
of condemned books, the other a collection of expurgations required in books
deemed obnoxious in part only. These
are known as the Quiroga Indexes, after
the Inquisitor-general of that day. Yet
other Indexes were issued in 1612, 1632,
1640, 1707, 1747 and 1790. The last,
known as the *Indice Ultimo*, contained
no such list of expurgations as its predecessors had done.

It was not sufficient to produce Indexes ;
it was necessary to see that the prohibited works were not read. The Inquisition employed agents to search the
bookshops and even private libraries.
But it was at the seaports and on the
French frontier that it was most vigilant.
Not only packages of books were examined, but all sorts of merchandise—for

the Hernández episode was never forgotten. On the arrival of a ship in harbour its crew, passengers and merchandise were all liable to search by the Inquisition's commissioner. These *visitas de navios* were vexatious, for they entailed both delay and expense, the agent charging fees for his services. Constant complaints were made by merchants, especially at Bilbao, the principal port on the Biscay coast, and these complaints were backed up by the ambassadors of foreign Powers —but all to no purpose. The State fully approved of the inquisitorial system for the protection of the people from the poison of noxious literature, and its own Press laws were exceedingly drastic.

One slight mitigation of the censorial system was permitted. Heretical books must be not only burnt but refuted, and they could not be refuted without being read by someone. It was customary, therefore, to issue licences to persons the soundness of whose faith was beyond suspicion, allowing them to read, and occasionally even to possess, prohibited works. But licences were issued only after close inquiries into the character of the applicant and the object of his application, and they were not often granted.

193

What was the effect of the Press censorship maintained in Spain by the Government and the Inquisition ? It has been urged in its defence that the Spanish people were left free to read great masses of literature, in comparison with which the total of prohibited works was negligible ; that but few of the great Spanish classics appear upon the Index ; that there was no attack upon imaginative literature and no censorship of the drama ; that no philosophic or scientific works of a high order were proscribed ; that there was no narrow exclusion of original speculative literature ; that if the Roman Congregation condemned the works of Galileo, the Spanish Inquisition did not ; that there was no proscription of Averrhoës, Ramon Lull, Ficino, Copernicus, Descartes, Hobbes, Newton, Leibniz, Spinoza ; that all that the system did or attempted to do was to prevent a comparatively few books hostile to the Church and dangerous to the faith from falling into the hands of the uneducated and uninstructed.

All this may be true, yet the believer in the freedom of the Press will on the other hand urge that the censorship introduced into the realm of letters and into the book-trade the same sort of insecurity that confiscations of property by the Inquisition involved in business generally. Authorship and scientific inquiry were alike discouraged, and Spain in some measure at all events was kept isolated from the intellectual currents of the outside world.[1]

[1] For a full discussion of the topics summarily treated in this chapter see Lea, *Inquisition of Spain*, Vol. III, pp. 480–549 ; Vol. IV, pp. 95–335.

CHAPTER IX

THE SPREAD, THE DECADENCE
AND THE
ABOLITION OF THE SPANISH INQUISITION

THE activities of the Spanish Inquisition were not confined to the Peninsula ; they extended to most parts of the Spanish empire, though not to all. Neither in Naples, nor in the Milanese, did it prove practicable to establish a tribunal owing to the strength of hostile public opinion.

The papal Inquisition had been introduced into the kingdom of Naples when it belonged to the House of Anjou. There was much for a tribunal to do, since Waldenses from Piedmont had established themselves in Apulia and Calabria, and in course of time Jewish fugitives from Spain found a refuge in southern Italy. When Ferdinand of Aragon conquered the kingdom and the armies of the Great Captain, Gonzalvo de Córdova, had finally ousted the French, the new ruler was anxious to establish an efficient Inquisition on the Spanish model. The Neapolitans were no less anxious to avoid this, while they had no objection to the continuance of the existing not very energetic tribunal. Gonzalvo advised delay. Ferdinand, however, came to the conclusion in 1509 that he could now safely introduce the Spanish Inquisition. He soon found himself mistaken. So much excitement was caused by the mere rumour of his intention that he had to content himself with ordering the banishment of all Jews and Marranos. There was no such hatred of the Hebrew race in Naples as existed in Spain, and the order was not properly carried out until 1540, in the reign of Charles V. The papal Inquisition continued to function but was so little formidable that the most gifted of Spanish Protestants, Juan de Valdés, was able to settle down in Naples in 1534 and to spend the remainder of his life there without molestation, the centre of a little group of like-minded spirits such as Bernardino Ochino.

The Duchy of Milan remained in Spanish possession from 1529 till 1707. Philip II contemplated bringing in the Spanish Inquisition, but popular hostility was so strong that·he had to abandon the project. The papal tribunal did not work very satisfactorily until the saintly Carlo Borromeo became Archbishop of Milan, in 1561, when he threw the same passionate energy into the work of extirpating heresy within his diocese that he did into every duty which he undertook; but this story has no connection with the Spanish Inquisition.

Sicily in the fifteenth century was part of the dominion of the House of Aragon, but when the Inquisition was established in his kingdom Ferdinand did not immediately plant it in the island. In 1478, however, Torquemada dispatched an inquisitor thither, and as the edict of 1492 against the Jews extended to Sicily involuntary baptisms resulted, followed by the almost inevitable crop of Judaizing heretics. Many complaints were brought forward in Sicily against inquisitorial methods such as the extraction of evidence by excessive torture; the burning of persons who persisted up to the last in maintaining their innocence; the injustice done to widows whose dowries were not exempted when their husband's property was forfeited; the appointment of nobles as familiars; the excessive privileges accorded to familiars; the multiplication of officials. Something was done to satisfy the critics both by Charles V and by

Philip II, at any rate so far as the grievances relating to the familiars were concerned. But bickerings between the Sicilian tribunal and the civil authorities continued, and the local inquisitors claimed that the charges forced upon them seriously interfered with the efficiency of their work. In 1713, the island passed into the hands of the Duke of Savoy; by him it was exchanged for Sardinia five years later, when it became a possession of the Emperor Charles VI. Despite these changes the Sicilian Inquisition remained subject to the Suprema. In 1735 Austria had to cede the island, together with Naples, to Don Carlos, the future Charles III of Spain. He obtained from the Pope a special Inquisitor-general for Sicily, so that the connection with the Spanish Inquisition was at length severed.

Of the Sardinian tribunal little need be said. The Inquisition was introduced into this possession of the House of Aragon before the close of the fifteenth century. It was employed against Conversos with some energy during its early days, but it seems to have been exceptionally prodigal in the appointment of familiars and useless underlings, and the most outstanding feature of its history down to its extinction, when the island was handed over to the Duke of Savoy in 1718, is the almost incessant disputes with the State regarding matters of privilege.

In 1505 a tribunal was established in the Canary Islands, but at first it had little independence, being under the control of the tribunal at Seville. The islands had attracted a considerable Jewish population owing to the absence of the Holy Office : nevertheless it was not until the tribunal had become independent and a particularly energetic inquisitor had appeared in Grand Canary that there was much persecution. Soon after his landing at Las Palmas—in the autumn of 1569—a great *auto* was held, which attracted spectators from the other islands of the group. There were indeed twice as many spectators as the whole population of Grand Canary. While there are a good many cases of relapse into Judaism on the part of the Jewish contingent in the Canaries and of relapse into Mohammedanism on the part of baptized Moorish slaves, the majority of the offences brought before the Inquisition are those of solicitation in the confessional, blasphemy, and sorcery. But much the most interesting proceedings are those against foreign heretics, most often

English, Dutch or Flemish, of which there are a considerable number in the last decades of the sixteenth century.

Both regular traders and filibusters sometimes found their operations in these Spanish seas a hazardous business. The authorities were happy to capture *corsarios luteranos*, and seamen, who were first brought before the civic magistrates as pirates, were liable to find themselves handed over subsequently to the Holy Office as heretics. The majority of these seafaring men were willing to compound with their captors by abjuring their religion, and only one Englishman was so obdurate as to be brought to the stake— a certain George Caspar, who perished at an *auto* in 1587. Profession of Catholicism did not always bring release, as at any rate one Dutch Calvinist found who, on expressing a desire to be received into the Catholic Church, was dispatched to a convent in Spain so that he might be instructed in his new faith, and with strict injunctions never to enter a heretic country again. On the other hand, escapes from the islands were not infrequent and little or no trouble was taken to recover fugitives. Escaped or liberated prisoners carried back to England terrible tales of

201

the Spanish Inquisition—and its ill-fame there was in no small measure derived from their descriptions of the dungeons of Las Palmas; but bitter complaints of such deprivations and discomforts as having to drink wine diluted with water and of a dietary of fish, green vegetables and oranges do not suggest serious ill-usage. But if very few of these foreign heretics were burnt many of them were tortured, while their ships and their merchandise were forfeited.

The advent of the Inquisition followed the introduction of the Spanish power into America. In Mexico the bishops seem to have exercised the effective control over heretical causes until the reign of Philip II. When the Inquisition was properly established it at once became very active, and owing to its great distance from the mother-country it was perforce largely independent of the Suprema. Of the early victims a large proportion were foreigners. Thirty-six of Sir John Hawkins's men fell into the hands of this Mexican tribunal. Owing to lack of provisions during the course of his third voyage in 1567, he had to land half his crew on a hostile coast, and of these one Miles Philips has left an account of the *auto* at which he was present. Several Englishmen were burnt at the stake in Mexico and these punishments and the much more frequent public floggings of the hated heretic pirates gave great satisfaction to the Spanish population.

There are the usual cases of bigamy, blasphemy, seduction, and superstition; and in the seventeenth century there was an outburst of persecution against Portuguese Jews; but much the most interesting episodes in the later history of the Mexican Inquisition are the prosecutions of two leaders in the War of Independence of 1808–15. Miguel Hidalgo, priest of Los Dolores, led out his parishioners in revolt in 1810. He was a man of remarkable physical and intellectual powers, not very squeamish in matters of moral conduct, and not at all reluctant to express dangerously unorthodox views in public. Twice already he had been denounced to the Inquisition for his disorderly life and his blatant errors, but the evidence was contradictory and no action was taken. When, however, he appeared as a leader of revolution, catalogues of all the manifold offences which had ever been attributed to him appeared in the churches, and he was summoned to appear before the Holy Office. Since he was engaged in military operations against the Government he did not of course present himself, and in his absence he was solemnly charged with being both a deist and an atheist, both a Judaizer and a Protestant, a blasphemer and a seducer—indeed with well-nigh every crime in the inquisitorial calendar. In 1811 Hidalgo, who was no general, was defeated and captured. The civil authorities kept him in their custody, and eventually executed him, but while he was lying in prison he addressed a long letter to the Inquisition, protesting his submission to the tribunal and elaborately vindicating himself against the accusations of heresy. The Inquisition did not know whether to accept this confession or not, and merely suspended the case indefinitely, as the easiest way out of a quandary.

Morelos, like Hidalgo in Holy orders, was a more successful military leader, but he also eventually proved unsuccessful. Unlike Hidalgo, he was, when captured, lodged in the secret prison of the Inquisition, and tried by that tribunal before the secular authorities started their proceedings, which it was a foregone conclusion would terminate in his execution. The inquisitorial trial was hustled through in four days—no doubt because the civil power was impatient. He was found guilty of being a deist and an atheist, a follower of Hobbes and Voltaire—the formula was almost as extensive as in the case of Hidalgo—and he was degraded from the priesthood before being delivered up for his trial as a traitor to the State.

As in Mexico so also in Peru jurisdiction over heretical causes was first maintained exclusively by the bishops, and it was not until 1570—thirty-five years after the completion of the conquest by Pizarro—that the Inquisition was introduced into the country. The territory over which the new tribunal—stationed at Lima—assumed responsibility was immense, for it included not only Peru but Chile and indeed the whole of Spanish South America. Commissioners were established at Buenos Aires and at Santiago de Chile, but even so the radius of effective jurisdiction must have been very limited, and the possibilities of escape from the clutches of the Inquisition considerable. New Granada (i.e. Colombia and Venezuela) was cut out of the viceroyalty of Peru in 1563, and a separate tribunal was established at Cartagena in 1610 ; but subsequent suggestions for the creation of yet another tribunal in South America were refused on the ground of expense.

There does not seem to have been much for the Inquisition to do in South America. There, as in Mexico, the natives whose conversion was undertaken by many zealous missionaries, were as a rule left alone. Philip II enjoined special treatment for them on the ground of their insufficient grounding in the faith, in an instruction of 1572. It was the comparatively small European population from whom the heretics came, and it was not until there took place an incursion of Portuguese Jews that heretics became at all numerous or their persecution at all profitable. The great majority of the offences brought before the tribunals at Lima and Cartagena were those in which heresy was merely inferential. A number of mystic impostors were dealt with in the early seventeenth century—notably Angela Carranza, whose reputed miracles, ecstasies and revelations for fifteen years deceived the whole human race in Peru from viceroys and archbishops downwards. The influence of the natives is no doubt to be discerned in the large number of cases of culpable superstition which were brought before the tribunal at Cartagena, and if heretics were not found among the natives a good many witches were.

There are a few cases of foreign Protestants being captured before the Inquisition. Among them was John Drake, a cousin of Sir Francis Drake, who after being shipwrecked on the Pacific coast and spending a year among the Indians made his way across the continent to Buenos Aires, where he was seized and sentenced to reconciliation and to confinement in a convent for three years. In 1594 Richard Hawkins, son of the great Sir John, was severely wounded and captured by the Spaniards at San Mateo. Most of his men were sent to the galleys at Cartagena ; but he himself and a dozen others were conveyed to Lima, where they were claimed by the Inquisition and consigned to its dungeons. Eight of them appeared at an *auto* in December, all professing conversion and being reconciled, with the exception of one William Leigh, who was sentenced to six years of the galleys followed by perpetual imprisonment, Hawkins, who was too ill to be present at the *auto*, was sent to Spain, where he was imprisoned from 1597 till 1602. There are one or two cases of the burning of English heretics by the Lima tribunal. The need for making special efforts to deal with heretical foreign seafarers was urged by the Council of the Indies before the end of the sixteenth century. It had been suggested that there ought to be a tribunal at San Domingo to have jurisdiction over the West Indies, but the proposal was not adopted.

While it is important to note the extension of the sphere of influence of the Spanish Inquisition as the result of the spread of the Spanish empire both in Europe and beyond the Atlantic, from first to last the main theatre of its operations remained the Peninsula itself. It was in its earliest days, those of Torquemada, that the Holy Office was most sanguinary; in those of Ximenes, Adrian of Utrecht, Manrique, Valdés, Espinosa and Quiroga it was at the height of its fame. But if it reached its zenith during the reigns of Charles V and Philip II, it may perhaps be said to have been even more powerful under Philip IV, inasmuch as that sovereign showed towards it a deference which was almost subservient. To all appearances the Inquisition was as influential as ever under the unhappy Charles II, and never was there an *auto* celebrated with greater pomp than that of

1680 at Madrid, when there were **100** victims.

But with the advent of the Bourbon dynasty at the opening of the eighteenth century there came a marked change. Philip V refused to attend an *auto* on his accession, and while he was persuaded that the Inquisition was too useful an aid to the royal supremacy not to be favoured by the Crown, he and his successors were determined not to permit the existence of an *imperium in imperio*. This may indeed be said also of Ferdinand and Charles V, but the French sovereigns, if not more masterful than they, were just as absolutist in their policy and a great deal less sympathetic to the Inquisition. A prince who had been nurtured at Versailles thought of the Court as necessarily a centre of culture and enlightenment, and the coming of the Bourbons led to the inauguration of learned academies and learned journals in Spain. The new tendencies visible under Philip V were still more marked under Ferdinand VI, and most of all under Charles III, who is generally reckoned as one of the " philosopher kings," and who was surrounded by ministers possessed of an outlook essentially secularist, tolerant and utilitarian.

In the new atmosphere the Inquisition had to walk warily. It could no longer be contemptuous of criticisms of its irregular and arbitrary proceedings and its unjustified immunities, and Llorente tells us that the eighteenth-century inquisitors were very different from their predecessors, being models of sweet reasonableness and leniency. The spirit of the age, reflected in the attitude of the Court and the ministers, was too strong for the Inquisition ; it no longer possessed the authority and respect that it had hitherto enjoyed, and many of its scantily-paid officials grew slack and indifferent. When it acted with its old assurance it met with no support from the educated classes and even sometimes with popular hostility. Some high-handed proceedings on the part of the tribunal at Alicante led to the suggestion, brought forward in 1797 and the two succeeding years, that the Holy Office should be abolished.

But there was no real chance of its decease at that time, for the outbreak of the French Revolution had given the Holy Office a new lease of life. The anticlerical and indeed at one time atheistical character of the movement in France filled the great majority of Spaniards with horror and strengthened the innate conservatism of the national character. The Inquisition became once more, for a brief period, the symbol of Spain's time-honoured possessions—the unsullied purity of her faith, her monarchical government and the sacred rights of property. Thus when in 1798, Grégoire, the republican Bishop of Blois, called upon Spain to abolish the Inquisition, to overthrow despotism and to establish toleration, the only result was the publication of zealous replies in defence of Spain's monarchy and of her Inquisition, in which the bishop was reminded that the fall of man was a much more pregnant fact than that of the rights of man.

When in 1808 the armies of Murat and Junot placed Joseph Bonaparte upon the throne of Spain the Suprema supported him in Madrid. But when Napoleon himself arrived there in December a decree was issued abolishing the Inquisition and declaring its property forfeit to the Crown. Its archives were handed over to the custody of Antonio Llorente, who had been secretary of the Madrid tribunal from 1789 to 1791. He, with a precipitancy which did more credit to his humanity than to his qualifications as an archivist, burnt all the records of criminal cases which came into his hands save any which he adjudged to be of special historical importance, such as those of Carranza and Froilan Díaz. But Napoleon's edict did not mean the extinction of the Spanish Inquisition any more than the victories of his armies meant the extinction of Spanish independence. Wherever the French were kept at bay the tribunals continued to function.

From the autumn of 1810 the national resistance to the French was directed by a Cortes at Cadiz, a body representing only the unconquered parts of the country, and filled with men who were honest and liberal-minded but inexperienced. From the first the Cortes embarked upon a domestic policy which threatened the existence of the Inquisition. Its decision in favour of the principle of a free Press deprived the Holy Office of its censorship and at the same time unmuzzled a number of enemies of the institution, such as Antonio Puigblanch, who, under the queer pseudonym of Natanael Jomtob, wrote at this time his *La Inquisition sin Máscara*. But the Holy Office had its defenders, who argued as of old that Spain had been saved from such disasters as Lutheranism and Voltaireism by its intolerance ; and

212

those who were now hostile to it were denounced as Jacobins.

Early in 1813 the Cortes, after prolonged and acrimonious discussion, voted by a large majority that the Inquisition was inconsistent with the new liberal constitution which it had adopted, and that jurisdiction over heresy should rest with the episcopal courts. It ordered that a statement justifying the discontinuance of the Inquisition should be read in all parish churches on three consecutive Sundays. This was an impolitic step. The verbose manifesto in which the decay of the country was attributed to the influence of the Inquisition gave widespread umbrage, though the city of Madrid congratulated the Cortes on putting an end to the activities of an institution which had transformed men into tigers and prevented the progress of the arts and sciences in Spain.

This discontinuance of the Inquisition lasted less than eighteen months. The restoration of Ferdinand VII to his throne was a severe set-back to the cause of Spanish liberalism. He, indeed, took an oath to uphold the constitution of 1812, but he was an utterly base and despicable creature, and his word was no security for anything. Surrounded as he was by " men of Gothic ideas," as Llorente terms them, he was soon persuaded that the restoration of the Inquisition was necessary alike for the welfare of religion and the strengthening of monarchical authority. On May 4, 1814, he declared all the proceedings of the Cortes of Cadiz null and void, which meant the sweeping away of the constitution of 1812 and, implicitly, the revival of the Inquisition; and on July 21 the King announced that the tribunals were to resume their functions. He explained that the revival was necessary, owing to the evil done to religion by the presence in the country during the Peninsular War of so many heretical foreign soldiers.

The last chapter in the history of the Inquisition was of brief duration. The misgovernment of Ferdinand gave rise to one conspiracy after another. At last in 1820 the revolt led by Rafael de Riego and Antonio Quiroga was successful, and on one and the same day—March 9—the King renewed his oath to the constitution of 1812 and issued a decree abolishing the Inquisition. But the new régime was neither popular nor successful, while the King chafed at the restrictions imposed upon him. When in 1822 the representatives of the Great Powers assembled at

Verona to discuss the current problems of Europe, Spain had once more been reduced to anarchy. With the approval of Russia and Austria, though not of Great Britain, a French army, under the command of the Duc d'Augoulême, entered Spain and, meeting with only the feeblest resistance, in April 1823 restored Ferdinand to the full exercise of royal power. At once the King issued decrees invalidating everything that had been done since March 1820. Did that involve the restoration of the Inquisition ? In the absence of any definite ruling on the subject one or two of the tribunals resumed their minor activities in a tentative way.

But the Inquisition was not restored. It was made abundantly clear to Ferdinand that the French, to whom he owed his salvation, were strongly opposed to such a proceeding. Chateaubriand, who had been the chief inspirer of the expedition, protested emphatically against any such tarnishing of the victory achieved by French arms. The persecution of heresy in the Peninsula was not, however, quite ended, and episcopal courts, under the title of *Juntas de fe*, with the secrecy of procedure which had been characteristic of the Inquisition, exercised jurisdiction

215

in matters touching the faith. The last execution for heresy ever witnessed in Spain took place on July 26 1826, when a poor schoolmaster of the highest character, named Cayetano Ripoll, was hanged as an unrepentant deist. He was buried in unconsecrated ground, his body being encased in a barrel upon which scarlet flames were painted, in order that modern practice might at any rate symbolically be made to accord with ancient precept. Another forty-three years elapsed and Spain passed through the miseries of the Carlist Wars and the reign of the infamous Isabella II before, on June 6 1869, the principle of religious toleration was for the first time introduced into her constitution.

CHAPTER X

To very many people the Spanish Inquisition seems a byword for revolting cruelty. It was an object of intense loathing to generations of Englishmen. When Spain was the national enemy in the sixteenth century, English traders and buccaneers, who had been incarcerated in its secret prisons and subjected to its tortures in the Peninsula itself or upon the Spanish Main, brought home with them lurid stories of its horrors. When anti-popish fanaticism ran high in the latter half of the seventeenth century it was still further excited by the publication of such accounts of the Holy Office as Dugdale's *Narrative of Popish Cruelties*, Beaulieu's *The Holy Inquisition* (with an appendix devoted to the Popish Plot), and Dellon's *History of the Inquisition as it is practised at Goa*. To eighteenth-century rationalism, whether French or English, the Spanish Inquisition appeared

217

to be an insane barbarity.[1]   In the nine-teenth century the best-known historians writing in English about Spain, such as Froude, Motley and Prescott, were openly hostile to the Roman Catholic Church, while the majority of books written speci-fically about the Spanish Inquisition were essentially propagandist in tone and often little more than laudations of the Protest-ant martyrs of Spain. Very little at-tempt was made prior to the last half-century, either on the Catholic or the Protestant side, to form a dispassionate estimate of either the Papal or the Spanish Inquisition.

We cannot hope to understand the phenomenon of the Holy Office, we can-not even account for its existence, unless we make an effort to appreciate the point of view of those who founded and of those who fostered and maintained it. The case for the Spanish Inquisition was put, not very successfully, by De Maistre in

[1] Voltaire's abhorrence is expressed in his well-known verses :
Ce sanglant tribunal,
Ce monument de pouvoir monacal,
Que l'Espagne a reçu, mais elle-même abhorre :
Qui venge les autels, mais qui les déshonore ;
Qui, tout couvert de sang, des flammes entouré,
Égorge les mortels avec un feu sacré.

his famous *Lettres à un Gentilhomme Russe sur l'Inquisition Espagnole*; with great ability by Balmez in his *Protestantism and Catholicism compared in their Effects on the Civilization of Europe*, and in Menéndez y Pelayo's *Historia de los Heterodoxos Españoles*.

Their arguments may be summarized as follows. Tolerance is the easy virtue of the sceptic who neither believes nor hopes in anything. In the era when the Spanish Inquisition was founded and flourished everybody believed in something and therefore everybody was intolerant. Such Protestants as Calvin and Queen Elizabeth both approved of and practised persecution. But for the Catholic the question of the treatment of heresy goes much deeper than those considerations of mere political expediency which appealed to Queen Elizabeth. To him it appears axiomatic that wrongful opinions are as justly punishable as wrongful acts; indeed more so because evil deeds are simply the inevitable outcome of evil thoughts, and a man's behaviour is the reflection of his character, while his character is moulded by his conceptions of his duty towards God and his fellow-men which we term religion. Heresy, which means wrong ideas of religion, is therefore a grave crime as well as a sin, because it compromises the very existence of civil society, which is ultimately founded upon a true apprehension of God and righteousness. Toleration where vital matters of the soul are concerned is mere indifference to the fundamental disparity between truth and falsehood, right and wrong. If it be objected that we cannot be sure of what is truth and what is right, the answer is that no one who accepts the Christian revelation can have any doubt in this matter. The Church, absolutely assured that she stands upon foundations of rock, has an authority so firmly established, so absolute, that there can be no room for qualms as to her right to uphold the truth and to punish those who rebel against it.

It is not only the Church that has appreciated the fundamental heinousness of heresy. Ever since the code of Theodosius the secular power had always held that the individual ought not to be free to discuss theological questions and to hold any opinion that happens to appeal to him, for it recognized that theological questions are never merely academic, but vitally concern the political organism, if only because the right ordering of the life of the family, which is essential for the welfare of the State, is dependent upon sound religious principles.

The Inquisition is often associated with the idea of barbarous cruelty, as though the use of torture were peculiar to it. It is true that the Inquisition in Spain habitually used torture and was reputed to be particularly successful in pressing the truth out of people's bones, as Cervantes puts it in *Don Quixote*; but it merely utilized the same sort of methods of extracting evidence as were customary in secular tribunals, not only in Spain, but in Protestant Scotland, for example, where the thumb-screw and the boot were still applied by the courts in the seventeenth century.

The *odium theologicum* enters a great deal into discussions of the Spanish Inquisition, and the Roman Catholic Church is attacked because of the cruelties practised by the tribunals. But in the sixteenth century, as Balmez argues, when all nations used fire and sword to settle religious questions, it gave no shock to the prevailing ideas of the time to find religious dissidents being made to suffer for their opinions. One of the most brilliant Spanish men of learning of that age who suffered for heterodox views was Servetus, but he was burnt not in Spain but in Calvinist Geneva, and his execution was approved by Melanchthon and Beza. In 1612 Edward Wightman and Bartholomew Legate were found guilty of holding heretical opinions and burnt at Lichfield and Smithfield respectively. Protestant England raised no protest against those proceedings. An ordinance of 1648 against blasphemy made all those who denied the divinity of Christ, the doctrine of the Trinity, or the existence of a future state liable to the death penalty. The fact that no executions followed the issue of this ordinance does not alter the fact that the attitude of its Puritan authors was not far different from that of Torquemada. While the Spanish Inquisition was on the whole singularly rational in its treatment of witchcraft, holding the stories of the Sabbat to be a delusion, Protestant Scotland atrociously tortured and burned to death thousands of unhappy women reputed to be witches. We shudder at the thought of the penalty of the stake : let us remember that as late as the year 1726 a woman named Catherine Hayes was burnt alive at Tyburn for the murder of her husband. If we are harrowed by the description of the secret prisons of the Spanish Inquisition, were they any more dreadful than the English prisons before Howard began his movement for their reform ?

Such considerations as these are not merely relevant, but essential, to a true understanding of the Spanish Inquisition, because we cannot view any institution in proper perspective if we view it in isolation. Nowhere is it more necessary to remember the parable of the beam and the mote than in the study of the history of religious persecution. Defenders of the Spanish Inquisition are entitled to use the " tu quoque " argument against a good many of their adversaries.

They are also justified in repudiating the very common view, expressed in Prescott's phrase that Spain in the sixteenth century was a country " shut out from the light," that in the period when the Inquisition was most powerful Spain was in consequence of its intolerance a land of ignorance and obscurantism. Such an idea is indeed a quite grotesque travesty of the facts, and it can be based only upon ignorance, the truth being that the sixteenth century

223

was the age of Spain's greatest glory in the sphere of thought as well as of action. Salamanca and Alcalá were among the great universities of Europe. Of the humanist scholars of Europe none save Erasmus himself, who greatly admired him, was more brilliant than Juan Luis Vivés. Francisco Sánchez was only less distinguished. Domingo de Soto, a predecessor of Grotius, and Francisco Suarez, were the greatest masters of jurisprudence of their day, and the latter, " the prodigy and oracle of this age," as he was called, was a philosopher and theologian. There were also such remarkable thinkers among the Spanish Jesuits as Molina and Fonseca. Indeed in classical learning, theology, philosophy and law Spain produced some of the most original and remarkable men of the century. The succeeding epoch may have been an era of political decline ; but it was no decaying culture that produced *Don Quixote*, the greatest poems of Lope de Vega, the dramas of Calderon, and the masterpieces of El Greco, Ribera, and Velasquez.

It is a mistake to think of the inquisitors as necessarily men ignorant of, or hostile to, learning. Ximenes, founder of the University of Alcalá and editor of the polyglot Bible, was one of the most learned men of his age; Manrique and Sandoval were friends of Erasmus; Valdés was the founder of the University of Oviedo; Quiroga also was a distinguished scholar. If the Inquisition undertook the censorship of books, it was but performing a function undertaken by the State in Spain and all other countries—at least down to the end of the seventeenth century and in most cases much longer. The Spanish Inquisition was not, argues Menéndez y Pelayo, hostile to culture; it was the preserver of culture—of the distinctive religious-minded civilization of the country against the insidious dangers of alien and subversive elements within, against the intrusion of noxious destructive forces from without. The Holy Office helped to maintain not only true religion but sound thinking, to keep at bay the pernicious Protestant fallacy of predestination, which in belittling the freedom of the individual is inimical to the development of the personality necessary for the attainment of greatness in all the imaginative arts and in the highest sciences. " Wherever Lutheranism reigns, there letters are destroyed," said Erasmus. Spain, defending herself alike against the schism

225

of Germany and the licence of Italy, was the chief agent in the reformation of the Church from within, in the great work which she accomplished at the Council of Trent, and by producing in the Company of Jesus a great moral and intellectual force, which re-established the great principle of the freedom of the will, reorganized education, placed the sciences once more under the ægis of religion and purged the Renaissance of its paganism. The Inquisition is to be regarded as the third of Spain's great contributions to the war upon intellectual anarchy and to the reform of the Church. The moral standard of the clergy, both regular and secular, in Spain was higher than elsewhere, partly because of the zealous energies of Ximenes, Pedro of Alcántara, Juan de le Cruz and Santa Theresa, but partly also because of the dread power of the Inquisition which assailed not only the heretical layman but also the peccant priest.

An attempt has been made to reproduce faithfully the delineation of the Spanish Inquisition presented by its ablest advocates. Let us now look at the reverse side of the picture. It should in the first place be noted that even its most earnest defenders nowadays do not attempt to justify all its proceedings. Modern humanitarianism renders such a course quite impossible. There are features in the history of the Spanish Inquisition which cannot be commended to the conscience of the modern world by any conceivable pleading. An attempt at a complete defence must inevitably defeat its own object. Judged by an enlightened standard many of its proceedings must necessarily be condemned; it is only by relating them to the standard of a past age that they can be excused. While it is essential to adopt an historical approach to such a subject as the Spanish Inquisition and to try to appreciate points of view which are at all events strange and possibly even repugnant to us; on the other hand, we must not allow ourselves to waver in our own standards and permit a sympathetic treatment of ideas of a past age to degenerate into the casuistical process of " making the worse appear the better cause." There were indignant critics of the abuses of inquisitorial practice at every stage of its history, and if their strictures accord with enlightened conceptions of right and justice, it must follow that their criticisms

227

were just. If we leave out of consideration the attacks of contemporary Protestants on the ground that they were due to religious bias, and of contemporary competing jurisdictions on the ground that they arose from jealousy, we are still left with the censures of good Catholics who were actuated by no such motives —for example Mariana, who criticized the cruelties inflicted upon the innocent by the Inquisition's methods, and Cervantes, who, in the famous chapter in *Don Quixote* where the priest examines the books in the knight's library, and in sundry other passages, poured ridicule upon its methods of censorship, its ignorance and credulity.

The principal significance of the Holy Office in the domestic history of Spain lies in the persecution of the Moors and the Jews. It was an instrument for the harrying of those who had been forced to accept an alien religion in which they often received but little instruction and which in such circumstances they had little cause to love. The hostile spirit adopted towards these races under Ferdinand and Isabella led to the expulsion of those who remained true to their old faith, and rendered life intolerable for the converted. It brought to an end the friendly intercourse between the races which had, despite the Moorish wars, upon the whole prevailed during the Middle Ages, and rendered impossible any unity of hearts. The policy of proscription, while it contributed temporarily to the royal exchequer, impoverished the country by driving out some of the most industrious and thriftiest elements in the population, and by denuding the public offices and the professions of many of the ablest and most adaptable of its inhabitants. To a king such as Philip II the religious uniformity of the country seemed of more consequence than its economic welfare. Religious uniformity was preserved, but at the heavy price of industrial deterioration.

The declension of Spain, often attributed to the existence of the Inquisition almost as a matter of course requiring neither argument nor demonstration, was in fact due primarily to a weak industrial system and a very mistaken economic policy, to " an incapacity for economic affairs which seemed almost inspired." [1] Large tracts of country, particularly in Castile, were barren ; agriculture even when conditions

[1] R. H. Tawney, *Religion and the Rise of Capitalism* (1926), p. 72.

were favourable was apt to be neglected ; and the accumulations of the precious metals from the Peruvian mines raised the price of commodities among a people who were mainly peasant cultivators. These evils were augmented by the expulsion of non-Christian inhabitants, which was not due to the Inquisition, but was merely another manifestation of the same intolerant spirit that produced the Inquisition. It is at the same time quite true that the Holy Office did do economic harm by its system of confiscations. The automatic forfeiture of the property of the heretic appealed to the Crown, for it enriched the royal revenues as well as providing for the maintenance of the Inquisition ; but it was only a short-sighted view that could regard such constant private calamities as profitable to the State. They were indeed a pernicious kind of capital levy, which deprived the country of resources necessary for its development, while inevitable uncertainty as to the identity of those upon whom this sort of blow would next fall was prejudicial to credit and to the confidence which is the very life-blood of commerce.

Another of the evils in Spanish life to which the Inquisition undoubtedly contributed was the deplorable conceptions of *limpieza* and *mala sangre*.[1] The worship of the former established the most pernicious system of caste imaginable. Uncontaminated blood counted for more than ability, so that the country was prevented from making the best use of its natural resources in human capacity. Modern philanthropy regards with concern the permanent slur which is cast upon a wrong-doer, and after he has expiated his offence aims at helping him to make a new start in life as a decent member of society. The Inquisition not only completely blasted the careers of the guilty, but penalized generations of innocent descendants. Thus damage was done both to the community at large and to many unhappy homes.

Again, it is vain to argue that no harm was done to the intellectual development of Spain by the Inquisition and its system of censorship. It left open a good many fields for inquiry and speculation, but it quite definitely closed others. Intellectual activity was conditioned and directed

[1] In the printed catalogues of all the business which came before the Toledo tribunal, 330 pages are devoted to trials of heresy, bigamy, etc.; 348 to investigations into *limpieza*.

by a force which was concerned not with progress but with restrictions and inhibitions. The bold adventurous mind was subjected to the repressive influence of those who, if they did not actually look askance at adventure, at all events had no desire to encourage it. It was not safe to spread one's wings, to take part in investigation or controversy touching the ultimate problems of existence. Scholars who abhorred the very thought of heresy sometimes found themselves confined to prison for months and even years while their writings were submitted to the judgment of censors who were their intellectual inferiors. Such writers as Luis de Leon, Juan de la Cruz, El Brocense are cited to prove that the Inquisition did not harm the country's intellectual life. But all three and others like them were cited to appear before the Inquisition; some of them had their work interrupted by bitter periods of imprisonment and their peace of mind destroyed by the torture of an inquisitorial process. A system which subjected to such treatment some of the great writers and thinkers of whom Spain is now most justly proud was obviously prejudicial to science and letters. When men of great reputation and of unblemished life could be brought before the Inquisition perhaps for nothing worse than some incautious utterance, many must have drawn the moral that it was best to be silent and not to give expression to rash thoughts at all. Mariana, who criticizes the way in which the Inquisition caused suffering to the innocent, laments also the deprivation of freedom of speech which it entailed. Juan de Luna, writing in 1620 about the ignorance of his fellow-countrymen, regards it as excusable because the inquisitors are its cause. As the wind agitates the leaves, so the very name of the Inquisition causes everyone to tremble.

This brings one to perhaps the most odious feature of the inquisitorial system. It deliberately created and diffused an atmosphere of fear and of suspicion. By its Edicts of Faith it declared systematic delation to be a praiseworthy thing; by suppressing the names of witnesses it made it a safe and easy thing. It placed the distinguished at the mercy of the commonplace, the courageous at the mercy of the craven, the noble-hearted at the mercy of the malicious. The virtues of mutual trust, understanding and sympathy were discountenanced. Nay, more, it was an integral feature of the system that to incur suspicion became virtually a crime. It was almost impossible for a man to leave the tribunal before which he had been defamed without a stain on his character. The question which inquisitors decided was not " Guilty or Not Guilty ? " but " How far Guilty ? "

The characteristic features of the Inquisition's procedure clash with modern conceptions of fairness and reasonableness. The whole onus of proof was thrown upon the defendant, who was at the same time almost completely deprived of the means of effectively undertaking it. The pervading atmosphere of secrecy, the refusal to allow any intercourse between the prisoner and his relatives and friends, the suppression of the names of witnesses, the absence of really serviceable counsel, the lack of opportunity for cross-examination, the utilization of torture, the wearing and indeed nerve-racking slowness of the process—all these disabilities combined together made it excessively difficult for any accused person to establish his innocence. There was only one avenue of escape which did not present almost insurmountable obstacles—to do what the Inquisition desired him to do, confess that the charges against him were true, declare himself penitent, and be reconciled.

To the majority of people the greatest infamy attached to the Inquisition is its use of the stake. It is true that the Holy Office repudiated all responsibility for the death of the heretic whom it handed over to the secular arm. But this repudiation was merely formal, and the authors of inquisitorial manuals and treatises had no hesitation in declaring that death by burning was the only right and proper penalty for the obdurate or relapsed heretic. The Spanish Inquisition showed less reluctance in bringing the culprit to the stake than either the Medieval or the restored Roman Inquisition, and although, as we have seen, the records do not allow of any estimate of the total figures of those who were burnt, we can say with certainty that in the early decades of the institution these were to be numbered in thousands. Holocausts admittedly were much more frequent under Torquemada and his immediate successors than at any subsequent period, and relaxations were few and far between in the era of the Inquisition's decay, yet at the best the Holy Office in Spain has a terrible record of destruction. Balmez, while approving the existence and the work of the **Spanish** Inquisition, considers that it could **have** effectively preserved the country from the dangers of Islam, Judaism and Protestantism without the use of the stake, and regrets that it should have afforded the enemies of Catholicism the opportunity of charging the Church with being guilty of blood.

It may, finally, be urged against the Spanish Inquisition that it was responsible for moral harm. In the first place, it sometimes tended to distort moral values. Priests who were found guilty of the singularly revolting crime of using the confessional for immoral purposes were lightly punished. It is true that the Inquisition was a tribunal for the trial of heresy and not of immorality; on the other hand, it endeavoured to obtain sole jurisdiction over these cases, and the result was that the offence met with inadequate penalties. In the second place, the spectacles which the Inquisition deliberately exhibited for the public warning or gratification—the floggings in the street, the horrors of the *brasero*—were as degrading to the onlookers as they were cruel to the sufferers. The pity of it is not that the Holy Office was no worse than secular tribunals, but that it should have been possible for it to be no better. It is horribly incongruous that such a system should have been administered by the ministers of Christ, and in His name.

But if we must needs apportion blame for such horrors let us be just. It was not the Inquisition alone that carried to dreadful extremes the consequences of the conviction of the supreme importance of orthodoxy. When Zwingli spoke in a glowing passage of the assembly together in paradise of all the saintly, the heroic, the faithful, of Abel and Enoch, Noah, Abraham and Isaac, together with Socrates, Aristides, Antigonus, Numa, Scipio and Cato, Luther despaired of Zwingli's own salvation. No age, no religion, no country has had a monopoly of cruel acts done from the highest of motives. The story of the Spanish Inquisition is dreadful, but it is more than that—it is tragic. Some of its officers may have been wantonly cruel or unworthy of what its best members regarded as a high calling; but there were, on the other hand, inquisitors of the finest character and the purest motives, who most earnestly believed that they were engaged in defending the Church of God and His Christ from the attacks

237

of the Devil. So also among the prisoners there were no doubt many who were most justly punished for perverse lives and noxious opinions, and some of higher character, who, whether sincere or not in the creed which they professed, proved, when the test came, of a poor courage; but there were others who persisted to the end and died martyrs to the cause of devotion to an inner conviction of truth. It is in the clash between men of nobility on either side, between different conceptions of truth, between the conflicting ideals of unity of religious faith and of intellectual integrity; it is in the pitifulness of the misunderstandings, the cruelties, the sufferings and the heroisms which arise from such spiritual antagonisms that there lies the enduring interest of the history of the Spanish Inquisition.

NOTE ON BOOKS

THE extant original records of inquisitorial trials are in the great Spanish archives of Simancas, Madrid, Barcelona, etc. Printed versions of some of the most important processes—e.g. of Carranza, Luis de Leon and El Brocense, are to be found in the *Colección de Documentos inéditos para la historia de España*, Vols. V, X, XI. Other extracts from these sources will be found in Lea's *History of the Inquisition of Spain* (see *infra*) ; J. M. Marin, *Procedimientos de le Inquisición* (2 vols., Madrid, 1886), Vol. II ; *Records of the Spanish Inquisition* (Boston, 1826), being extracts from the records of the tribunal at Barcelona.

Several important inquisitorial manuals are contained in Zilettus' *Tractatus Universi Juris* (Vol. XI, Pt. 11, Venice, 1584), e.g. Simancas, *De Catholicis Institutionibus*, with notes by Peña—an exhaustive compendium dealing with items of procedure, etc., in alphabetical sequence ; J. à Royas, *De Haereticis* ; Albertini (a Sicilian inquisitor), *Tractatus de agnoscendis assertionibus catholicis et haereticis ;* Lopez de Palacios, *Allegatio in Materia Haeresis* ; Villadiego, *Tractatus contra Haereticam Pravitatem*.

See also Ludovico à Paramo (another Sicilian inquisitor), *De Origine et Progressu Sanctae Inquisitionis* (Madrid, 1598), Book II of which is devoted to the history of the Inquisition in all parts of the Spanish dominions. For the medieval papal Inquisition in Aragon the great authority is Nicolas Eymeric, *Directorium Inquisitorum* (Rome, 1585 ; Venice, 1607). Peña, who annotated many of the inquisitorial treatises, wrote one himself under the title of *Inquirendorum Haereticorum Lucerna* (Madrid, 1598).

The earliest hostile account of the Spanish Inquisition is Gonzalés de Montés, *Inquisitionis Artes Detectae* (Heidelberg, 1567). Translated into several European languages before the end of the sixteenth century, it did not appear in Spanish till 1851. The English version (1569) has as its title *Discovery and Playne Declaration of Sundry Subtile Practices of the Holy Inquisition of Spayne*. Many strongly Protestant accounts appeared in the seventeenth and eighteenth centuries—e.g. R. Dugdale, *Narrative of Popish Cruelties* (Harleian Miscellany, Vol. VII) ; *History of the Inquisition with an account of the Cruelties exercised therein*, and similar pamphlets to be found in Brit. Mus. Tracts 866g, 6 and 7 (cf. also " The Loyal Martyrs," *Roxburghe Ballads*, Vol. III, p. 605) ; L. de Boileau, *The Holy Inquisition* (1681) ; J. Marsollier, *Histoire de l'Inquisition* (English trans. by Chandler, 2 vols. 1731) ; John Marchant, *A Review of the Bloody Tribunal . . . of the Inquisition* (1770). J. A. Llorente wrote his famous and very hostile *History of the Inquisition* in Paris. Original French version, 1817 ; English, 1818 (Abridged, 1826) ; Spanish, 1835–6. Also very hostile, A. Puigblanch, *La Inquisición sin Máscara* (1811)—English trans., 1816 ; W. H. Rule, *History of the Inquisition* (1866).

The standard modern history is H. C. Lea's monumental *History of the Inquisition of Spain* (4 vols., 1922). See also his *Chapters from the Religious History of Spain* (1890) ; *The Inquisition in the Spanish Dependencies* (1908) ; and, for the medieval Inquisition in Spain, *The Inquisition of the Middle Ages* (3 vols., 1887), Vol. II, pp. 162–90. Allowance must be made for Lea's pronounced anti-Catholic bias, but nothing at all comparable in intensive scientific research has been done on the other side, and all later books on the subject, such as the present one, are inevitably indebted to it. See articles by S. Reinach in *Revue Critique* for 1906, 1907, 1908. There is a very readable popular account of the early days of the tribunal in R. Sabatini, *Torquemada, and the Spanish Inquisition* (1913).

For the Roman Catholic point of view consult J. M. de Maistre, *Lettres à un gentilhomme russe sur l'Inquisition espagnole* (1844); J. Balmez, *Protestantism and Catholicity compared* (English trans., 1849); Menéndez y Pelayo, *Historia de los Heterodoxos Españoles* (3 vols., 1880–1); R. Cappa, *La Inquisición Española* (1888).

For the Moriscos see Comte Albert de Circourt, *Histoire des Maures, Mudejares et des Morisques* (3 vols., Paris, 1846); D. F. Jance, *Condición social de los Moriscos en España* (Madrid, 1857); H. C. Lea, *The Moriscos of Spain* (1901).

For the Jews : A. de Castro, *History of the Jews in Spain* (English trans., 1851); J. Amador de los Rios, *Historia social, política y religiosa de los Judios de España y Portugal* (3 vols., 1875–6); J. Jacobs, *An Inquiry into the Sources of the History of the Jews in Spain* (1894); E. N. Adler, *Auto de fe and Jew* (1908).

Among the numerous works on Spanish Protestantism the following may be recommended : M. Geddes, *Spanish Protestant Martyrology* (1730); T. McCrie, *History of the Progress and Suppression of the Reformation in Spain* (1829); A. de Castro,

Spanish Protestants and the Persecution of Philip II
(English trans., 1851); C. A. Wilkens, *Spanish Protestants in the Sixteenth Century* (English version, 1897); E. Schäfer, *Beiträge zur Geschichte des Spanischen Protestantismus* (3 vols., Gütersloh, 1902); E. Boehmer, *Bibliotheca Wiffeniana : Spanish Protestants of two Centuries* (3 vols., 1874–1904). The last is the most valuable.

For the Mystics : P. Rousselot, *Les Mystiques Espagnols* (Paris, 1867); E. Allison Peers, *Spanish Mysticism* (1924); *Studies of the Spanish Mystics* (2 vols., 1927, 1931); A. F. G. Bell, *Luis de Leon* (1927); J. Cuervo, *Fray Luis de Granada y la Inquisición* (Salamanca, 1915); R. P. P. Dudon, *Le Quiétiste Espagnol Michel Molinos* (Paris, 1921); P. S. Rodriguez, *Introducción á la Historia de la Literatura Mistica en España* (Madrid, 1926), esp. pp. 246–56.

For the Censorship : Reusch, *Der Index der verboten Bücher* (3 vols., Bonn, 1883–5).

For the Inquisition in the Spanish Dependencies : Lea (*ut supra*); J. T. Medina's works published in Santiago de Chile on the Inquisition in Chile (2 vols., 1890); in Cartagena (1899); in the Philippines (1899); and on the primitive American Inquisition (2 vols., 1914); *Documentos inéditos . . . para la Historia de Mexico* (Vol. XXVIII, 1910 ; A. B. Wallis Chapman, *English Merchants and the Inquisition in the Canaries* (1912); L. Amabile, *Il Santo Officio della Inquisizione in Napoli* (2 vols., 1892).

The following works may also be consulted for the religious history of Spain : A. Bernáldez, *Historia de los Reyes Catolicos* (Seville, 1870); H. del Pulgar, *Cronica de los Reyes Catolicos* (Valencia, 1780); G. Zurita, *Anales de la Corona de Aragon*

(6 vols., Saragossa, 1610); D. Ortiz de Zuñiga, *Anales eclesiásticos . . . de Sevilla* (Madrid, 1677); J. de Mariana, *General History of Spain* (English trans., Stevens, 1699); W. H. Prescott's *History of the Reign of Ferdinand and Isabella* (3 vols., 1871) and *History of the Reign of Philip II* (3 vols., 1855); M. A. S. Hume, *Spain, its Greatness and Decay* (1899); R. Altamira y Crevea, *Historia de España y la Civilización española* (4 vols., Barcelona, 1913)—abridged English version, *History of Spanish Civilization* (1930); and his *La Psicalogia del Pueblo español* (Madrid, 1902); A. Ballesteros, *Historia de España* (5 vols., Barcelona, 1918–29); R. B. Merriman, *The Rise of the Spanish Empire* (3 vols., 1918–25).

INDEX

INDEX

INDEX

INDEX

248

INDEX